CHEESE

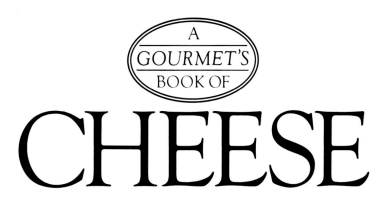

A GOURMET'S BOOK OF

CHEESE

CAROL TIMPERLEY
&
CECILIA NORMAN

Photographed by
GRAHAM TANN

a Salamander book

Published by Salamander Books Limited
LONDON • NEW YORK

Published 1989 by Salamander Books Ltd,
52 Bedford Row, London WC1R 4LR

This book was created by Merehurst Limited
Ferry House, 51/57 Lacy Road, London SW15 1PR

© 1989 Salamander Books Ltd

ISBN: 0 86101 402 2

Distributed by Hodder and Stoughton Services,
PO Box 6, Mill Road, Dunton Green,
Sevenoaks, Kent TN13 2XX

Commissioned and Directed by Merehurst Limited
Managing Editor: Janet Illsley
Editors: Maureen Callis, Renny Harrop and Elizabeth Martyn
Recipes by: Cecilia Norman, Carole Handslip, Dolly Meers
and Kerenza Harries
Photographer: Graham Tann
Stylist: Sue Russell
Home Economists: Dolly Meers and Annabel Hartog
Designed by Peartree Design Associates
Typeset by Angel Graphics
Colour reproduction by Kentscan, England
Printed in Belgium by Proost International Book Production, Turnhout

ACKNOWLEDGEMENTS

The publishers would like to thank the following
for their help and advice:
John Cavaciuti Delicatessen, 181 Hornsey Park Road,
London N8; Harvey and Brockless, 44/54 Stewarts Road,
London SW8; James Aldridge, 188 High Street, Beckenham,
Kent; Jeroboam's, 26 Bute Street, London SW7; The London
Cheese Company Ltd, Unit 9, Cedar Way, London NW1;
David Mellor, 4 Sloane Square, London SW1;
Jim Vale, Singleton's Dairies, Longridge, Lancs.

Companion volumes of interest:
A Gourmet's Book of VEGETABLES
A Gourmet's Book of HERBS & SPICES
A Gourmet's Book of FRUIT

Contents

Introduction

The art of the cheesemaker is one of delicate balance. To produce a perfect cheese, with the right depth of flavour, the most mouth-watering texture and delicious aroma, depends on many factors. The milk – from cow, ewe or goat – the breed of animal and the type of pasture all have a bearing on the end result. So too do the complexities of making and maturing the cheese.

To enjoy good cheese is to enjoy variety, contrast and subtlety. There's a cheese for every palate and for every occasion, from the mildest, blandest types, through a whole range of rich, mellow and buttery flavours, to the most pungent, sharp and salty cheeses at the far end of the flavour spectrum. Then there's an astonishing choice of colours and textures to enhance eye and palate. From firm handsome Cheddars through to crumbly, pale Wensleydales; from the soft white curds of Ricotta, to the oozing nature of ripe Brie or Camembert. Veined cheeses, charcoal coated, wrapped in leaves, enriched – the delights to be discovered are endless.

Cheese originated as a money-conscious way of using up surplus milk, and different countries have developed their cheese-making and eating habits in different ways. The French serve it after the main course, before dessert; a habit which is becoming increasingly popular elsewhere. Italian pasta wouldn't be the same without a scattering of Parmesan; while the mild crumbly cheeses of England melt obligingly to make a wonderfully smooth Welsh rarebit.

With so many types to choose from, cheese can be enjoyed in an infinite variety of ways. Savour it to the full by itself, with bread or biscuits, or as a partner for fruit. Complement it with a glass of wine; or let it add its own special note to a hundred-and-one different dishes. However you use it, cheese belongs in a class of its own.

Choosing Cheese

Cheese, like wine, is one of life's great pleasures. Pierre Androuet, the doyen of French cheese, even goes so far as to say, If I had a son who was ready to marry, I would tell him 'Beware of girls who don't like wine, truffles, cheese or music.'

Sadly, it is one which is all too often unheeded and many an otherwise enjoyable meal is marred by badly chosen, ill-kept and ill-matched cheese and wine. Yet with just a little thought and care, a cheeseboard can be the highlight of a meal, capable of compensating for any culinary lapse.

The trick is not to be over ambitious. Tiny slivers of a dozen or more cheeses are neither appetizing nor complementary: too many flavours and textures all competing for attention merely become confusing and result in a lot of dried-out, unusable left-overs. For an average-sized dinner party of six people, four cheeses are more than adequate and the possibility of serving just one superb cheese alone should never be discounted.

Quality should always be the first consideration when selecting cheeses. It is worth seeking out a good cheesemonger whose stock is kept in carefully controlled conditions. A shop like this will be able to advise you on your choice and should have a wide range of clearly labelled cheeses on offer, including more unusual varieties. Always ask to taste first before you make your decision – a reputable cheesemonger will be delighted to oblige. Be flexible in your selection: if the Brie you'd set your heart on isn't up to scratch, substitute a Camembert or a Coulommiers.

The first rule of shopping for cheese is never to buy anything in less than prime condition. Ask for your portion to be freshly cut and look first at the cut surface of the whole cheese. It should have a fresh appearance, and no tell-tale sweatiness, cracking or hardness, all of which indicate that the cheese is drying out.

It's a good idea to feel soft cheeses if you can. They should be springy to the touch and when ripe should be evenly soft from centre to edge. Check that soft cheeses are not too runny. Smell is another good indicator of quality, so sniff your sample of cheese before you taste. It should have a fresh smell, redolent of its particular variety. Reject any that have a hint of ammonia, as they are past their best.

Selecting for a cheeseboard

Here you should address yourself to the question of balance. A cheeseboard should sit comfortably with the other courses of the meal, which means taking into account the type of food being served (is it strong and spicy, light and fresh or somewhere in between?); the wines which will accompany it; and the relationship between the cheeses themselves. The single, most important factor is never to serve cheeses which require a lighter wine than that which has been drunk with the main course as this has a nasty, jolting effect.

This, of course, assumes that you will serve the cheese before the pudding, French-style. The reason for this is that few cheeses consort happily with sweet dessert wines; most need something drier or fruitier to offset them to advantage.

Texture, as well as flavour, needs careful thought. The ideal cheeseboard includes at least one hard or semi-hard cheese, perhaps a traditional English cheese like Cheddar or Cheshire; one semi-soft cheese, which could be one of the milder, washed-rind cheeses; one very soft cheese, perhaps a chèvre or a bloomy-rind specimen; and the fourth possibly a milder blue or a cheese with a *cendre* coating.

Cheeses should always be eaten in ascending order of strength to be fully appreciated. And it's worth noting that soft, semi-soft and blue cheeses are tasted by pressing them against the palate with the tongue, while hard or sharp cheeses are tasted on the tip of the tongue. In this way variations in consistency and flavour are apparent. If you think your guests may be uncertain about which cheese to try first, then unobtrusive numbered labels are quite a helpful idea.

Cantal *(hard)*

Murol *(semi-soft)*

Bucheron *(chèvre)*

Roquefort *(blue)*

An appropriate selection for a cheeseboard.

Storing Cheese

Overall, it is best not to buy a larger quantity of cheese than you can reasonably eat within a couple of days. This ensures that you will enjoy the cheeses at their best. If you should happen to acquire a whole cheese it may be possible to keep it for more than a year, uncut. It's a tricky business however, as the cheese must be kept in the correct conditions, in a cool, moist, ventilated room; and needs regular turning and wiping if it is not to deteriorate.

The length of time a cheese can be kept depends on its moisture content. Fresh cheeses which are high in moisture should be used within a couple of days. Take note of the sell-by date if you buy these cheeses in sealed cartons. Once it is past, the cheese will soon start to go off. Keep near the top of the refrigerator in the carton, or in a plastic bag.

For most other cheeses, the vegetable drawer of the refrigerator provides the best temperature for storage. Soft bloom-rinded cheeses, like Brie or Camembert, should be kept in their boxes or on a plate.

Cover the cut sides only with plastic wrap. These cheeses should not be stored for more than a few days. Semi-soft to hard cheeses keep for longer and the hard grating cheeses like Parmesan, either grated or as a piece, will keep for several weeks. Wrap all these cheeses tightly in foil or plastic to keep out the air. (Use freezer layer tissue rather than cling wrap.) Different types should be wrapped separately and strong tasting varieties should be kept away from bland foods. If mould spots develop, cut them off. They will not affect the rest of the cheese.

Cheese which has been bought sealed in plastic may begin to sweat. Remove plastic and blot the cheese dry with kitchen paper before rewrapping in plastic tissue wrap.

Remove cheese from the refrigerator 1-2 hours before serving so that it has time to reach room temperature. Cheese bought for same-day consumption can be kept under a cheese dome, although these should not be used for longer storage. Prop the lid up slightly to allow water vapour to escape.

Cooking with Cheese

Cheese is a very versatile ingredient and adds interest and flavour to all manner of dishes including sauces, soufflés, dips, quiches and pizzas. It can be used in baking, and deep-fried it makes a delicious starter in its own right. Of course, cheese is not limited to savoury recipes, for it can be successfully used in cheese-cakes, mousses and other sweet dishes. The selection of gourmet recipes in this book explores the versatility of cheese to its full.

As with wine, it is a mistake to assume that poor quality cheese will undergo a radical metamorphosis once heated. The better the quality of the cheese, the better the finished dish will be.

Careful cooking pays dividends, because cheese separates at 65.5°C/150°F and if cooked for too long becomes leathery and tough. When melted on its own it tends to become stringy and the texture is better if the cheese is mixed with a starchy food, such as breadcrumbs or potato, or added gradually to a sauce. Hard cheese cooks better if it is first grated, although crumbly cheese can be added to a recipe in small chunks. Avoid ready-grated cheeses of the type found in super-markets, however. These are impregnated with a non-caking agent and although convenient, quickly lose any flavour they once had.

Some cheeses melt better than others. Crumbly varieties such as Lancashire, Stilton or Cheshire are good in soups; while smooth types like Mozzarella and Bel Paese melt down to a pleasingly elastic consistency for pizza toppings. A finely grated hard cheese like Parmesan is perfect for sprinkling on soup or pasta, because the fine particles melt readily and mix into the dish so easily.

Cheddar is an excellent all-round cooking cheese, which grates well and gives a good flavour to sauces and soufflés. Soft cheeses such as Brie or Camembert add interest to quiches, and you can use Leicester or Double Gloucester to add colour. Stilton keeps its characteristic flavour when cooked and melts well. Gruyère and Emmenthal are the classic fondue cheeses.

Mozzarella is the classic pizza topping.

Presenting a Cheeseboard

Valençay (a cendré) is served on a separate board.

A carefully balanced, well-displayed cheeseboard, with a selection of appetising accompaniments, makes a perfect pause before dessert at a dinner party besides being guaranteed to revive the appetite of most diners.

It's worth taking time to arrange the cheeseboard attractively, although there's no need to overdo the decoration. There are two key facts to remember: the first is that cheeses are attractive in their own right (or should be if you've chosen correctly); and the second is that they are living, breathing organisms which require oxygen.

Despite the fashion for wooden or marble boards, you can present cheese on almost any material, provided it has a large enough surface area to allow air to circulate between the cheeses and prevent them from impregnating each other with smells. For this reason the very best way to serve cheese is on a wicker tray, which may be lined with leaves or straw ripening mats to protect it. Because blue and *cendré* cheeses are by their very nature dominant, it is best always to isolate these on a separate surface if possible. Likewise, provide a separate knife for each type of cheese. If the same one is used for all, the cheeses will not retain their individuality.

The overwhelming temptation to treat a cheeseboard like a still-life arrangement is to be discouraged. A few grapes between the cheeses are acceptable, but no more. Arrange the cheeseboard an hour or so before the meal and stand it, covered with a lid or piece of muslin, in a cool, but not cold, place.

Accompaniments

What to eat with cheese is another thorny subject. Bread or biscuits? Buttered or unbuttered?

Washed-rind and blue cheeses are probably best eaten just as they are, with a knife and fork, but many people prefer an accompaniment of some sort with other types.

A good solution is to offer a choice of bread or crackers. Fresh, crispy bread in the style of *pain de campagne* is the ideal, preferably flashed in the oven to refresh its crust just before serving. Rye and black breads or brown and Granary breads are other possibilities. Creamy cheeses can also be good with a light fruit or nut bread.

A selection of plain crackers, Bath Olivers, Scottish oatcakes or semi-sweet wheatmeal biscuits should provide something to suit most tastes. Butter is purely a matter of personal preference, but remember that it does have a tendency to dilute the flavour of the cheese. Always go for unsalted butter; salted is more assertive and interferes with the individual characters of the cheeses.

If a hard English cheese is included in your selection you could also offer a jug of celery. A bunch of grapes, or bowl of apples are other refreshing additions to the table.

A simple, effective arrangement of cheeses on a wicker tray lined with vine leaves, accompanied with grapes, celery and a selection of breads and biscuits.

Drinking Companions for Cheese

Cheeses vary so much in flavour that any attempt to suggest accompanying wines appropriate to each category is practically impossible. There are, however, certain characteristics common to each group which it may be helpful to consider.

Fresh cheeses are almost invariably soft in texture and delicate in flavour. This automatically rules out any wine which is strongly tannic as it will overshadow the cheese. Equally, very dry, flinty white wines are unsuitable with fresh cheeses as they create an unpleasant, acidic aftertaste. Something medium dry – white, rosé or an extremely light red – not only offsets the flavour of these cheeses to advantage but allows the palate to appreciate the nuances of their texture. Loire whites such as Muscadet and Sancerre, slightly chilled young Beaujolais or any of the new breed 'Blush' wines would be acceptable. If the fresh cheese is to be served as a dessert, with fruit, then a dessert wine such as Muscat or Sauternes would be delicious.

Bloomy rind soft cheeses like Camembert and Coulommiers can develop great depth of flavour which stands up well to most meaty full-bodied wines. Here red is the obvious choice, but by no means the only one. Chaource, for example, could just as successfully be partnered with Champagne or Chablis, while many experts believe that Brie and Camembert can happily collaborate with good farmhouse cider from Normandy. A more conservative choice, however, would be one of the less refined Burgundies, such as a Côtes de Beaune Villages, or any red made from the Pinot Noir grape.

Enriched or triple crème cheeses generally combine richness with a subtle strength which requires a correspondingly balanced wine. Something muscular, fruity and probably white is called for. Alsatian wines like Gewürztraminer have the strength to counteract the richness of these cheeses, yet being spicy, rather than dry, they do so without detracting from their subtlety. If red wine is preferred a Bordeaux or Cahors could be the answer.

Washed rind cheeses run the gamut of strengths, and it is more difficult to ascribe family characteristics to this group. A mild, sweet cheese like St Nectaire cries out for something crisp and white such as Sancerre, Pouilly-Fumé or any of the Upper Loire whites, while a cheese like Maroilles begs a wine with the body of a really top notch Burgundy. As the vigour of cheese increases, complement it with an increasingly dry wine.

Uncooked, pressed cheeses can, again, vary between delicate mildness and assertive strength. The former are generally best accompanied by good quality red table wine – nothing too elevated. The slight roughness of the wine adds interest to the cheese and can itself seem smoother and fuller for this foil. Almost any of the generic, supermarket own-label reds are suitable for this purpose. Here, white wines are probably best when tending towards fruit rather than bone dryness. Steer clear of Bordeaux and look instead to Alsace, the Loire, Australia, New Zealand and even England, though avoid anything 'thin'. Stronger cheese in this category can take much more distinguished reds as their relative sweetness has the effect of softening the tannin which can otherwise jar with cheese. Cheddar and Gouda, for example, can take both good Burgundy and some of the softer Bordeaux crus. Rich, dark ale produces the same effect at considerably less expense, worth bearing in mind if the cheese is being eaten alone, rather than as a course of a meal.

Hard, cooked cheeses almost all have a background sweetness of flavour which marries well with wine of any description other than bone dry, which inhibits this sweetness. Best of all is something full-bodied, fruity and white like a Beaujolais blanc, a Sauvignon or a good quality Alsatian Riesling or Gewürztraminer. Soft, warm reds are also good with these cheeses and the regions to look out for here are Savoie, Rousette and Chignin. Some of the better quality dark, rich beers should also not be discounted for hard cheeses.

Blue cheeses are, without exception, fairly salty and for this reason completely inappropriate with red wine, however mighty. All benefit a great deal more from being teamed with sweet white wines – controversial on the face of it but sensuously superlative. Roquefort with Sauternes and port with Stilton are both, rightly, classic combinations, but any good quality, sweet or sweetish white creates the same effect.

Goats' cheeses are traditionally accompanied by dry white wines, but again this is not an intransigent rule. Coarser, rustic reds can be equally satisfying provided they are not too full-bodied. Ewes' milk cheeses, on the other hand, can take something fruitier and livelier, because of their increased fat content. This also precludes anything

which is too tannic. Remember, tannin is to fat as oil is to water.

Soft cheeses with a natural rind have a different intensity of flavour, depending on whether they are coated in wood ash or allowed to develop natural moulds. The former are in general much stronger and require a fullish, red wine or spicy white to be enjoyed to full advantage. The latter, being more delicate, are at their best with a soft, fruity white or gentle, unassertive red.

There are no hard and fast rules about which wine should be served with which cheese, and the suggestions above should be taken as broad indications only. Humbler beverages like dark ale or cider should not be ignored: these can be admirable when matched with cheeses like Cheddar or Beenleigh Blue.

Personal preference is what counts above all and even experts don't always agree. Some, for example, think that a mature Cheddar served with sherry as an hors d'oeuvre is quite amusing; others deem this sacrilege. Imagination and the courage of conviction are all that really matter.

The classic combination: Stilton with port.

Fresh Cheeses

Fresh cheeses are simply non-aged cheeses which depend solely on lactic fermentation for their character. Cows', goats' or ewes' milk is rennetted or heated to encourage curd formation, excess whey is drained off and the curds are moulded or whipped to smoothness, according to the type of cheese. No further curing takes place. Fresh cheeses are prized for their delicate lactic sharpness and refreshing, moist texture.

COTTAGE CHEESE

A soft cheese, usually made from skimmed, pasteurized milk. After souring with added rennet, the curds are drained and washed. It has less whey extracted than most other cheeses, which accounts for its fairly liquid, granular consistency. Some brands have single (light) cream and salt added to improve the flavour. The end product is a bland, white, slightly acidic, low-fat cheese, much-favoured by slimmers and the cholesterol-conscious.

Cottage cheese can be eaten as it is, with crispbread, biscuits, bread or salad, or used as an ingredient in recipes, such as cheesecakes. It is sometimes sieved before use in cooking. It is also available with a variety of added ingredients, such as pineapple, chives, onions and peppers. These flavoured cottage cheeses make delicious sandwich fillings, with lettuce or watercress for contrasting texture.

CREAM CHEESE

Made in several countries, these cheeses are prepared from single (light) or double (thick) cream. To qualify as cream cheese they should contain more than 45% milk fat and are consequently quite rich. Cream cheese is recognized by its smooth texture and ivory colour. It can be used for spreading or piping, fillings and garnishes but is unsuitable for cooking as it has a tendency to separate.

CURD CHEESE

Curd cheese is made from ripened whole milk. It is unsalted and less rich then cream cheese: therefore it is more suitable for cooking purposes. It is sometimes known as lactic or acid curd cheese because of its slightly soured flavour. Consistency varies from fairly liquid to quite crumbly, according to drainage.

Curd cheese is used in cheesecakes and sweet and savoury fillings for flans, crêpes, etc. It is also a popular base for dips.

FETA CHEESE

Greece's most popular domestic cheese, Feta dates back thousands of years. The authentic version is traditionally made from unpasteurized ewes' milk, though occasionally from goats' milk or a mixture of the two. Commercial varieties (often imported from Denmark) are almost always made from pasteurized cows' milk which results in an altogether different – and inferior – cheese.

Real Feta is unfortunately difficult to sample outside Greece as demand there far outstrips supply; also, export restrictions on unpasteurized ewes' milk are stringent. Some small farms however do produce an acceptable version. The cheese has a crumbly-soft texture, white hole-flecked appearance and distinctive sharp, salty flavour. Often it is kept in brine to prevent dehydration. Feta is most frequently used fresh in salads, though sometimes it is used cooked, flavoured with herbs, as a filling for Mediterranean pastries.

Sussex Feta

Danish Feta

Greek Feta

Cream Cheese

Curd Cheese

Cottage Cheese

Cottage Cheese with chives

Fromage Frais – virtually fat free

Strawberry-flavoured Fromage Frais

Fromage Frais – 8% fat

FROMAGE BLANC OR FROMAGE FRAIS

French rennet curded cheese made from skimmed or whole cows' milk and whipped to achieve a smooth, thick consistency. Fromage blanc cheeses have a fat content of varying between 0% and 10%. Because of their versatility they are becoming increasingly popular. They can be used as a substitute for yogurt or cream in cooking and are superb sweetened and served with fruit as a dessert. Fromage frais flavoured with fruit, such as strawberry and apricot, is also available.

MASCARPONE

Sometimes spelt Maschepone, this unsalted cows' milk cheese from Italy has the consistency of soft butter. Snowy white in colour, it is ready to eat within twenty-four hours and is at its best during the autumn and winter months. Sold loose or in pre-weighed containers, Mascarpone may be eaten in its natural state or served as a dessert. It is particularly good when flavoured with chocolate, coffee, brandy or any liqueur. It has many culinary applications, notably in the preparation of pastries, desserts and vegetable dishes.

MOZZARELLA

A sliceable curd cheese from Italy made nowadays from cows' milk but originally from buffalos' milk. It is made by the *pasta filata* or spun curd method, which involves heating the curd in water until it becomes elastic and forms strands. These are wound into a ball after which pieces are cut from the curd and shaped.

Mozzarella is available throughout the year, loose or pre-packed but invariably suspended in brine to prevent dehydration. This cheese is used mainly for cooking as it has good binding properties. It is perhaps best known as the traditional pizza topping or in the classic Tomato and Mozzarella salad. It has a mild creamy flavour, pronounced lactic smell and immaculate white colour.

PANEER

A traditional Indian cheese widely available in Asian grocery stores. After coagulation the curds are strained and pressed into small, fairly firm blocks. Paneer, or *Panir* is not usually eaten in its natural state but used in the preparation of Indian sweets such as *rasgulla* and *rasmalai,* or grilled or sautéed .in vegetable curries.

Danish Mozzarella

Mascarpone

Italian Mozzarella

Petit Suisse

PETIT SUISSE

A rich cream cheese from France – although the name originates from the nationality of a worker in the cheese factory where it was developed, who used to transport the cheese to the Parisian markets. The cheese is made from pasteurized cows' milk enriched with cream to give a fat content of 60-70%. Unsalted and bland in flavour, Petit Suisse has a very soft, almost liquid consistency. It is made in portion-sized cylindrical shapes, sold paper-wrapped or in plastic containers. Petit Suisse can be used in the same ways as Fromage Blanc: in recipes served with fresh fruit; it is also similarly available flavoured with fruit.

QUARK

Quark is made in Germany, Holland, Great Britain and various other countries, and the spelling changes accordingly. The name simply means curds. It is virtually identical to a fromage blanc but with a slightly higher fat content – from 10-60%. In Germany it accounts for almost half the total cheese production, and the average German eats about 4.5 kg (10 lb) quark a year.

RICOTTA

A soft, white, crumbly cheese made from ewes' milk whey left over from the manufacture of Pecorino Romano. It is unsalted, relatively low in fat and at its best in the spring. Shaped like an upturned basin with a rough pattern on the outside, the curd is compacted so that the cheese can be cut with a knife. It may be eaten in its natural state, dressed with a light vinaigrette, or used as a filling for gnocchi or ravioli. It is sometimes used as a chocolate centre.

SAINTE-MARIE

A squat, cone-shaped cows' milk cheese from the Burgundy province of France, Sainte-Marie is thought to have been named after a feast day which falls in its best season: late spring and early summer. Made entirely on small farms from unpasteurized milk, it can be either salted or unsalted, but should always be creamy and supple rather than firm and crumbly in texture – the latter indicates that too much rennet was added to the milk. Pure white in appearance with a pleasantly sharp nose, Sainte-Marie's refreshing mildness is best appreciated when eaten alone.

Ricotta

Quark

Bloomy Rind Soft Cheeses

These cheeses are recognized by their reddish pigmented crusts dusted with white *penicillium* moulds and creamy-soft interiors. The degree of surface whiteness depends on the type of milk from which the cheese is made: unpasteurized milk encourages natural, off-white moulds while pasteurized milk cheeses are sprayed with artificial, toothpaste-white spores. Ripening occurs from outer rim to centre – usually within one to two months – and opinion differs as to the exact point of ripeness at which they should be enjoyed. As a rough guide, avoid very firm cheeses, which can be stodgy, and liquid ones, which have been insufficiently drained and can develop sharp notes.

BONCHESTER
Based on a traditional Coulommiers recipe, Bonchester is made in the border country of Scotland from the unpasteurized milk of Jersey cows. The cheese is strictly seasonal as it is made only with milk from grass-fed cattle. When fully ripe, Bonchester has a thick, buttery texture, deep yellow paste and sweet, balanced flavour. It is made in either 125 g (4 oz) or 315-375 g (10-12 oz) discs.

BRIE
The history of Brie stretches as far back as the 8th century when, according to legend, the French Emperor Charlemagne first tasted it at the priory of Reuil-en-Brie and thereafter insisted on regular supplies for the palace at Aix-en-Chapelle. While imitation Bries are made in many countries, to bear the name Brie legitimately the cheese must be made in the Seine-et-Marne area south of Paris. All Bries are made in flattish, disc forms of varying depths and ranging in diameter from 32.5-40 cm (13-16 in); their size influencing their development. A Brie in peak condition has a deliciously creamy flavour, very rich and fruity.

Genuine farmhouse Bries are imprinted with the marks of the straw mats on which they are ripened. Names to look out for include **Brie de Melun** with a salty, concentrated flavour, **Brie de Montereau** which has a mellow, rustic flavour and **Brie de Meaux,** the mildest of the three and regarded by many as the best Brie. Commercially-made Bries are less characterful but can be pleasingly mild. Many variations on the Brie theme also exist, such as Brie with peppers, mushrooms, walnuts, herbs and even blue veins.

CAMEMBERT
Camembert originated in the Normandy province of France and is named after a village in the Orne region where Marie Harel, a farmer's wife, perfected its recipe. Nowadays practically every European country and even the United States makes its own Camembert: none however can match the original, which relies on the salty richness of Normandy milk for its unique character. Smaller than a Brie, Camembert has a hearty, fruity flavour of great complexity. It is sold either whole, as a 13 cm (5 in) disc, halved or, in the case of factory-produced cheeses, in pre-packed individual portions.

CARRÉ DE L'EST
A square, pasteurized cheese from Champagne with a faint, musty aroma and bland flavour. It takes a mere three weeks to mature and it is very consistent in quality. The rind varies from white to orange depending on where the cheese is made.

Brie de Meaux

German mushroom-flavoured Brie

Camembert

Brie de Melun

Carré de L'Est

Bonchester

Chaource

CHAOURCE

A controversial cheese from the Aube *département* of southern Champagne, Chaource's unusual depth, about 7.5 cm (3 in) raises doubts about the uniformity of its development, which can vary considerably between crust and centre. Its virtues, however, lie in its refreshing flavour (superb when made from light, spring pasture milk), *chèvre*-like texture and excellent keeping qualities.

COULOMMIERS

Related to both Brie and Camembert, Coulommiers is neither as runny as the former, nor as strong as the latter. Creamy with a distinct fruity tang, the cheese has a nutty background flavour. Made in 13 cm (5 in) discs, Coulommiers is actually the name of the mould which gives the cheese its shape.

FEUILLE DE DREUX

Made from partially skimmed cows' milk, this rustic hand-ladled cheese from the Île de France is ripened in chestnut leaves. The surface moulds tend towards a blue-greyness rather than being white and the interior paste is a dull yellow colour. The flavour of this cheese is pronounced and quite fruity.

FOUGERU

A Coulommiers-type cheese ripened in bracken leaves. Larger than its prototype, Fougeru is approximately 23 cm (9 in) in diameter and weighs around 1 kg (2 lb). It is made exclusively on small farms in the Île de France, Champagne, Lorraine and Burgundy, from unpasteurized milk.

NEUFCHÂTEL

The chameleon of this group in that it changes its shape from manufacturer to manufacturer. Squares, briquettes and cylinders are all common, but romantics should seek out heart-shaped examples. Size and weight vary according to shape but an average cheese would tip the scales at around 100 g (3½ oz). Available all year round, these unpasteurized cheeses are at their best in summer and autumn when their salty smoothness is offset by a toothsome savouriness.

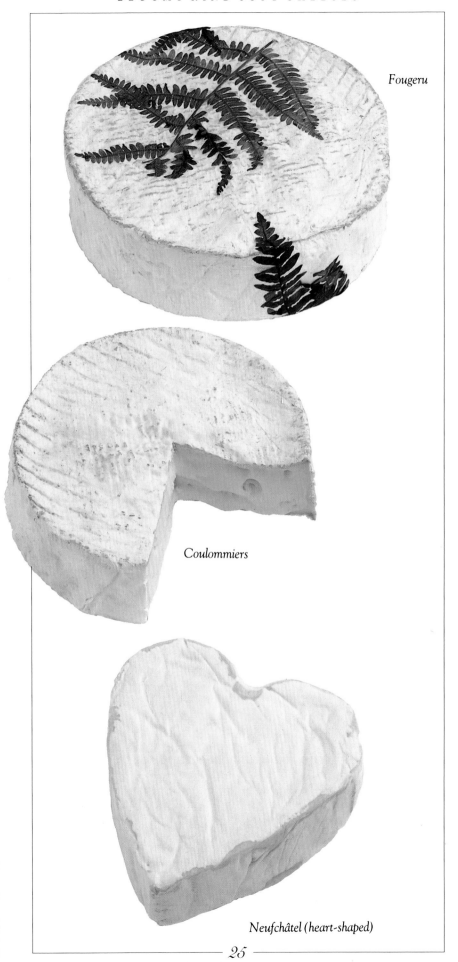

Fougeru

Coulommiers

Neufchâtel (heart-shaped)

Enriched Cheeses

Boursault

A branch of the bloomy-rind, soft cheese family which relies on the same manufacturing techniques, these cheeses are made from whole cows' milk, enriched with additional cream to raise their fat content from the standard 40-50% to around 75%. Though clearly not for the diet- or health-conscious, their buttery richness is countered by a deliciously rewarding depth of flavour.

BOURSAULT
A small drum-shaped French cheese, about 7.5 cm (3 in) in diameter, weighing 220 g (7 oz). Both pasteurized and unpasteurized versions of this cheese are available. Pasteurized cheeses are packed in a silver and white carton, unpasteurized ones in gold and white. Named after its creator, a cheese-maker based in St Cyr-sur-Morin earlier this century, the recipe is now owned by the Boursin concern. Boursault has a thin, bloomy rind and is creamy coloured. Rich and full-bodied in flavour, this cheese is best eaten when slightly runny.

BOURSIN
A native of Normandy and the Île de France, Boursault's commercial cousin is produced solely in factories from enriched, pasteurized milk. Plain Boursin can be rather disappointingly bland, but garlic, herb and pepper flavoured varieties are also made.

BRILLAT-SAVARIN
A relatively modern Norman cheese, invented by Henri Androuet in the inter-war years, it is probably true to say that this is the cheese by which all other triple crèmes are judged. Although soft, it is quite firm in texture with an appetizing nose and slightly sour, milky flavour. It is made in the form of a thick 13 cm (5 in) disc.

DÉLICE DE ST CYR
A carbon copy of Brillat-Savarin in every respect except that of flavour, which is milder with a nutty background. Délice de St Cyr is made in small factories in the Île de France and is a good buy throughout the year.

Brillat-Savarin

Boursin with Herbs

Boursin with Peppers

Explorateur

EXCELSIOR

A classic, speciality cheese made by small dairies in and around Normandy. It is a soft, double cream cheese with a fat content to match the triple crèmes – 72%. It is distinguishable by its irregular, cylindrical shape, dense firm texture and mild, almondy flavour. It is at its best during the summer and autumn.

EXPLORATEUR

Another Brillat-Savarin-type triple crème cheese which is smaller, firmer and milder than its prototype. It is made in small commercial plants in Brie country.

LUCULLUS

Named after Sulla's quaestor and consul who was renowned for his lavish style of entertaining, Lucullus is by no means an ancient relic but the product of the last decade. Unlike many cheeses, it reaches its prime during the winter when the cattle's more varied winter stall diet yields milk with a more complex, concentrated flavour, capable of withstanding the neutralizing effects of pasteurization. Made in commercial plants in the Île de France and Normandy, two sizes are available: the smaller weighs around 250 g (8 oz), the larger, approximately double. The latter is preferable as it develops more consistently.

MAGNUM

A pseudonym for Brillat-Savarin, which is the same cheese aged for longer.

PIERRE ROBERT

The creation of the Rouzaire family from Tournan en Brie, a highly respected and long-established line of dairymen and affineurs, Pierre Robert is another triple crème cheese to follow in the footsteps of Brillat-Savarin. In common with Lucullus, it is at its best when made from winter stall milk which lends the cheese an agreeable, almost salty sharpness. It has very little smell, being somewhat deeper than other related cheeses, which also accounts for its springy suppleness.

Pierre Robert

Lucullus

Washed Rind Cheeses

These are not dissimilar to bloomy rind cheeses in texture, being mainly soft and semi-soft. They have natural rinds which are washed, or sometimes soaked, in a solution of brine or alcohol to add flavour and facilitate ripening, which takes place in humid cellars. Their rinds are usually quite shiny and vividly coloured: the degree of apricot or red shading is determined by the duration and frequency of the washings. These cheeses do not sustain mould growth but their sticky surfaces attract cultures known as *bacterium linens* which aid development. Although they tend to be quite pungent – especially in hot weather – only the rinds smell (this is the reason they are seldom eaten); the interior pastes may be quite deliciously mild. Some cheeses, however, are through and through stinkers and definitely an acquired taste!

BERGUES

A low-fat, brine- and beer-washed cheese from the Flanders province of northern France. Bergues is made from skimmed cows' milk and has only 15-20% fat. Because of this, it is ideal for slimmers and a good keeper provided it does not dry out. Essentially a domestic cheese, Bergues is made by housewives and on small farms in either thick discs or flattened balls, 16.5-20 cm (6½-8 in) in diameter and 3.5 cm (1½-2 in) in depth. Curing takes places in humid cellars over a period of about two months. When ripe, the cheese has a smooth supple texture and mild flavour, with a hint of sharpness.

CHAUMONT

A small, cone-shaped cheese from Champagne with a depression at the top in which a puddle of brine collects during its two month curing spell. This seeps gradually into the cheese and produces a pronounced smell and robust spicy flavour. Chaumont's rind is very deeply coloured, ranging from brick-red to a deep red-brown. A whole Chaumont weighs around 220 g (7 oz) and should be supple, never soft, to the touch. It is at its best when made from spring and summer pasture milk.

COEUR D'ARRAS

As the name tells you, this strongly-flavoured, full-cream cows' milk cheese from Picardy is made in the shape of a heart. Like its close relation, Maroilles, it is washed in beer which gives it its striking red-brown rind. It has a soft supple paste.

DAUPHIN

Another relative of Maroilles, this crescent, heart or shield-shaped cheese is flavoured with tarragon and pepper. According to legend, it was named after the son of Louis XIV who, while visiting the French Hainaut province, was served a flavoured Maroilles which he greatly enjoyed. A dauphin weighs between 220-560 g (7-18 oz), depending on the cheese-maker, and is always approximately 3.5-5 cm (1½-2 in) thick. It has a smooth brown rind, fairly supple consistency and rather overwhelming nose. Again, it is at its best when made from luscious spring and summer pasture milk.

EPOISSES

A spicy, tangy, disc-shaped cheese from Burgundy which is washed in Burgundy marc. It has a strong bouquet and moist supple texture which ripens to the point of liquefaction. It is sometimes wrapped in paper leaves. Made from late spring and summer pasture milk, it has a three month curing period.

ESROM

A semi-soft, full-cream Danish cheese, formerly known as Danish Port-du-Salut. It has a creamy-yellow paste with many small, irregular holes and slashes. Rich and quite sweet when young, the cheese becomes much spicier and considerably stronger as it ages.

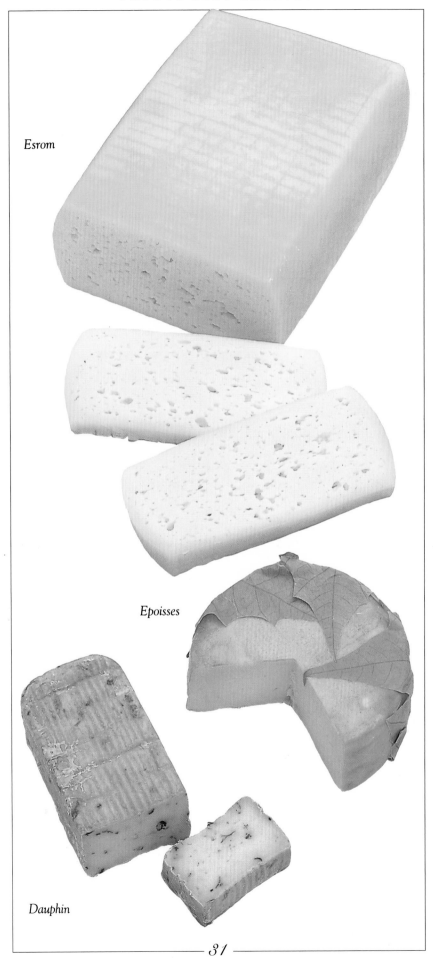

Esrom

Epoisses

Dauphin

Langres

LANGRES
A soft cheese shaped rather like a Yorkshire pudding with a concave surface to collect brine during washings which later diffuses into the cheese. It ripens to a rich deep flavour and creamier texture than most brine-washed cheeses. Langres has an apricot-brown rind and a wonderful spicy bouquet. It is made in the Champagne region and a whole cheese weighs between 280-345 g (9-11 oz).

LIMBURGER
A cheese of Belgian origin now also made in Germany and Holland. Made from cows' milk, it has a fat content of 30-40% (slightly lower than average). Thought to be a monastic invention dating from the Middle Ages, it is brick-shaped with an appropriately coloured brick-red rind. Pungent and spicy in both flavour and aroma, its fine-textured yellow interior tends towards suppleness.

LIVAROT
Made in the Normandy town of the same name, Livarot is thought to be a direct descendant of the Angelots of the past and was almost certainly invented by monks living in the region. It is sometimes called Livarot Colonel or the five-striper, a reference to the five bands of sedge which are traditionally used to hold it in shape. Nowadays, orange paper is often used in place of sedge. At its best from autumn to late spring, Livarot is a strong, spicy cheese, though rather less so than its bouquet suggests. It comes in the form of a small glossy brown cylinder 13 cm (5 in) in diameter, 5 cm (2 in) in depth and weighing 375-500 g (12 oz-1 lb). Its paste should be smooth and its texture resilient.

MAROILLES
A solid, reddish-brown, block-shaped cheese which was invented more than a thousand years ago by the monks of the Abbey of Maroilles. It is the oldest, best-known and most popular cheese of northern France. It is affectionately referred to as *le vieux puant* (the old stinker) in its home territory. While strong in flavour, it is by no means overpowering – the beer-washed rind is, again, the culprit. Its texture should be moist, not slimy, with few apertures in the paste. A contrasting fine white line running through the centre of the cheese is a good indication of ripeness.

MILLEENS
An Irish washed-rind, cows' milk cheese made solely at Eyries Farm, Bantry Bay, County Cork. It is a newly-established cheese, invented by philosopher Veronica Steele to utilize surplus milk supplies. Milleens owes much of its character to the natural bacteria which flourish in the ozone-rich atmosphere of this coastal area and which lend the finished cheese its sweet pungent flavour and moist creamy texture. A fairly large disc-shaped cheese, Milleens is at its best during the winter months when it ripens uniformly beneath its orangey-yellow rind.

Milleens

Livarot

Limburger

Maroilles

MUNSTER

An extremely popular cheese in Germany, Munster has been made in the Alsace region since the Middle Ages; both French and German varieties are produced. Munster is normally made in large disc shapes, about 20 cm (8 in) in diameter and 5 cm (2 in) thick. It is distinguished by its apricot-hued rind and semi-soft paste which is straw-yellow in colour. Smaller cheeses, 10 cm (4 in) in diameter are also made.

The two principal types of this cheese are **Munster Fermier** and **Munster Laitier**; the former is made by farms from unpasteurized cows' milk, the latter by commercial creameries from pasteurized milk. The fermier cheese is seasonal to summer and autumn, while the laitier is of consistent quality all year round. Brine-washed, munster has a smooth red-tinged rind, searing bouquet and extremely spicy, tangy flavour. A caraway seed-spiced kind is also made.

MUROL

A pretty pink ring-shaped cheese from the Auvergne province of France, made from pasteurized cows' milk and washed with brine. The cattle in this region are grazed on mountain pastures which are inaccessible during the winter months, making the cheese available only during summer and autumn. Cured for a mere six weeks, Murol has a bland inoffensive aroma and mild succulent flavour. It is quite supple in texture.

NANTAIS

Also known as Curé de Nantes, this is Brittany's most celebrated cheese. Invented by a Breton parish priest in the 19th century, it is made from cows' milk in small factories. Nantais comes in the form of a square shape with rounded corners, about 8 cm (3 in) square and 5 cm (2 in) thick. Its brine-washed rind varies from straw-yellow to deep ochre in colour, and it has a firm springy consistency and robust flavour. Though Nantais can be rather difficult to track down outside France, it is exported and well-worth searching for.

PONT L'ÉVÊQUE

Made almost exclusively on farms in Normandy from rich, salt milk, this is one of the oldest cheeses of the region; it was first recorded in the 13th century. A small, parallel-piped cheese with a dependable square base, it can be beige or orange in colour but should always be supple. The interior paste has a very soft texture and is pale yellow in colour. It has a pleasingly full-bodied flavour, with plenty of tang. Never buy Pont L'Évêque if it is runny.

REBLOCHON

A succulent farmhouse cheese from France's Haute Savoie *département*, Reblochon is the region's best-loved cheese – justifiably so, as it has a creamy, slightly aerated texture and a mild tangy flavour with background notes of nuts. Its crust can be either pale gold, apricot or deep orange: darker crusts indicate a stronger cheese. Consistency varies from firm to quite soft, particularly in summer when the cheese reaches peak condition; it remains there until early autumn.

REMOUDOU

Sometimes called Piquant, this is a Belgian cheese made from cows' milk in and around Liège by commercial dairies. Remoudou comes in trademarked, paper-wrapped cubes of about 7.5 cm (3 in) each weighing approximately 750 g (1½ lb). Its glossy, red-brown rind contains a powerful spicy cheese with lots of character and a very pungent aroma.

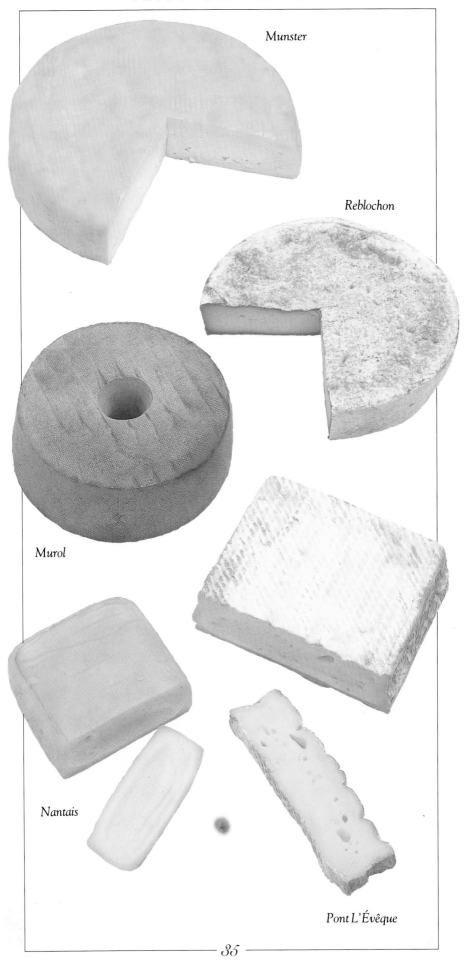

Munster

Reblochon

Murol

Nantais

Pont L'Évêque

SAINT-FLORENTIN

A soft, farmhouse cheese from the Burgundy province of France, Saint-Florentin is made from whole cows' milk and is washed with brine during its two month curing period. Made in the form of a flat disc about 13 cm (5 in) in diameter and 2.5 cm (1 in) thick, it has a smooth, shiny, red-brown rind and strong, spicy flavour with quite a noticeable tang. It is at its best from late spring until the end of autumn.

SAINT-NECTAIRE

A semi-soft, lightly brine-washed cheese from the Auvergne, Saint-Nectaire has been made since Roman times. It is made from mountain milk, redolent with the flavours and scents of alpine flowers and grasses. A mild, creamy cheese, it has a gentle tangy flavour and fragrant sweetness concentrated in its attractive red and mimosa-pigmented crust.

Saint-Nectaire is made in the shape of a disc, 25 cm (10 in) thick. Pasteurized Saint-Nectaire has a rectangular green plaque in its centre, the unpasteurized cheese has an oval one. Because it is made with milk from cattle grazed on alpine pasture, it is strictly seasonal and at its best mid-summer until the end of autumn. Saint-Nectaire is a distinctive, highly regarded cheese.

SAINT-PAULIN

An uncooked, pressed, French brine-washed cheese made by commercial plants from pasteurized whole cows' milk. The cheese has a smooth, thin orange rind and homogeneous, pale cream paste. Its mild delicate flavour is enhanced as the cheese ages, becoming quite tangy.

The cheese is best known abroad under the brand name Port Salut, though the original Saint-Paulin was in fact an ancient, monastic cheese. The cheese is cured for around two months and made in the form of a small, thick dinner plate. It is highly versatile but does not lend itself well to cooking.

SAINT-REMY

A small Munster-type cheese made in the Lorraine province of France. A square block-shaped cheese which weighs around 250 g (8 oz), it is cured with brine washings for six weeks. It has a smooth, light red-brown rind, penetrating nose and medium strength, spicy flavour. Made by local factories, Saint-Remy is best avoided during the winter months when it will be made from inferior quality milk.

SORBAIS

A Maroilles-style cheese from Flanders, Sorbais is just a shade milder. Made from whole cows' milk in slabs weighing around 750 g (1½ lb), it is ripened for three months. Its rind is smooth, shiny and reddish brown, with a strong, fruity bouquet and encloses a soft, yet supple paste. Like Maroilles, this cheese is often used locally to make a special kind of cheese tart, called goyère, and when cooked, the flavour of sorbais becomes surprisingly mild.

Saint-Nectaire

Saint-Paulin

Saint-Remy

Taleggio

TALEGGIO

Modern Taleggio is often a soft, bloomy-rinded cheese which bears no resemblance to the brine-washed original still made in Valsassina, a high, forested plateau in the Italian Alps. This has a strong, gutsy flavour redolent of sweet pasture. Made in 20 cm (8 in) squares 5 cm (2 in) deep, Taleggio has a thin pink or straw-coloured rind and ivory-hued, buttery interior.

TORVILLE

Made in England near Glastonbury Tor, which is reputedly the historical site of King Arthur's Camelot, Torville is actually Caerphilly washed with local Kneecracker cider. It is the Somerset pasture, however, rather than alcohol, which determines the nature of the finished cheese – sweet and fruity with an agreeable pungency. Torville is soft and creamy in consistency, but easily sliced. The rind is a rather dull orange shade.

TRAPPISTE DE BELVAL

A chunky, thick disc-shaped cheese about 25 cm (10 in) in diameter and 2.5 kg (5 lb) in weight, Trappiste de Belval is, by virtue of its size, an excellent cheese for keeping; it is brine-washed. A smaller 410 g (13 oz) version called **Dit D'Hesdin** is also made; this is washed in white wine. Trappiste de Belval is recognized by its pale apricot-hued rind, embossed with the marks of the jute cloth in which the cheese is wrapped before pressing. Properly matured specimens have girth rather than height and are moist, supple and agreeably mild.

VACHERIN

A generic name which covers a whole clutch of washed rind cheeses, hailing from the alpine regions of France or Switzerland. Vacherins are almost always larger than other washed rind cheeses; the smaller discs may weigh as little as 500 g (1 lb), but the larger wheels can tip the scales at 10 kg (22 lb). Production is by farms, dairies or picturesque chalets perched high in the mountains.

To categorize broadly, the larger cheeses are more supple than the tender, almost runny smaller ones. The colour of their rinds also varies within the paler shades of the spectrum. All are brine-washed and made from full-fat cows' milk. Larger cheeses are usually more predictable in quality.

Trappiste de Belval

Torville

Blue Cheeses

Blue cheeses, with their attractive, mould-veined appearance and creamy-white pastes, are prized for their complex, piquant characters. The vast majority of blue cheeses are made from cows' milk, some, including Roquefort – the king of French blues – from ewes' milk and others from goats' milk. They are sold either with a natural, dry rind, or with the rind pared away, in which case they are foil-wrapped to prevent dehydration.

They are uncooked, usually unpressed (though some are lightly pressed) and made from crumbled curds which have been sprinkled with *penicillium glaucum*. Once formed, the cheeses are perforated with wire needles to allow aerobic development of the mould veins through the cheeses, within the humid, natural bacteria-rich cellars in which they are cured.

Without exception, blue cheeses ripen from the centre to the crust and an even distribution of veins throughout is desirable. They are classed as soft cheeses and are characterized by their tangy, strong flavour and pungent aroma. However the strength of these cheeses varies considerably: not all are as strong as might be expected.

BEENLEIGH BLUE

One of the new breed of English farmhouse cheeses, Beenleigh Blue is made in Devon from the unpasteurized milk of Dorset/Friesland cross ewes. Since ewes, unlike cows, have only a six month lactation period and the cheese takes approximately seven months to mature, it is available only from mid-autumn to late spring.

At the beginning of the season, Beenleigh Blue has a pure white paste with light blue-green veining and is quite mild and firm. As the cheese ripens further, it becomes creamier with a more pronounced flavour. The cheese has a natural skin, and is wrapped in greaseproof paper. It normally weighs around 2.5 kg (5 lb).

BLEU D'AUVERGNE

A semi-soft cows' milk cheese from the Auvergne province of France, made both on small farms and by commercial dairies. Based on a traditional Roquefort recipe, the paste is pale yellow and quite sweet with an even distribution of sharply flavoured dark blue veins. The cheese is slightly greasy to the touch, has a powerful aroma and can sometimes tend towards saltiness. Again, it is made in 2.5 kg (5 lb) drums, which are foil-wrapped.

BLEU DE BRESSE

Often abbreviated to Bresse Bleu, this creamy soft cheese from the Pays de l'Ain is commercially produced from pasteurized cows' milk. Made in a variety of sizes in the shape of a cylinder, it is fairly richly flavoured and not dissimilar to a Dolcelatte. It is usually foil-wrapped.

BLEU DES CAUSSES

An open-textured, penetratingly-veined cheese with a delicious, concentrated creaminess. It is made in Roquefort country by commercial dairies, mainly from unpasteurized cows' milk, in 2.5 kg (5 lb) drums. Its best seasons are summer and autumn, when the cheese has been made from rich, fragrant summer pasture milk. The foil wrapper on every cheese bears a quality control label, guaranteeing its pedigree.

BLEU DE GEX

Thought by many experts to be one of France's most interesting blues, this natural-rinded, slightly pressed cheese is only rarely obtainable outside its native Pays de Gex and should be seized upon if sighted. Made by small farms and traditional dairies from full-fat, unpasteurized cows' milk, its unique delicate flavour is redolent of alpine flowers – the cows graze on high pastures above 2,000 metres (6,000 ft). A flat, disc-shaped cheese with convex sides, it weighs between 5-6 kg (11-13 lb).

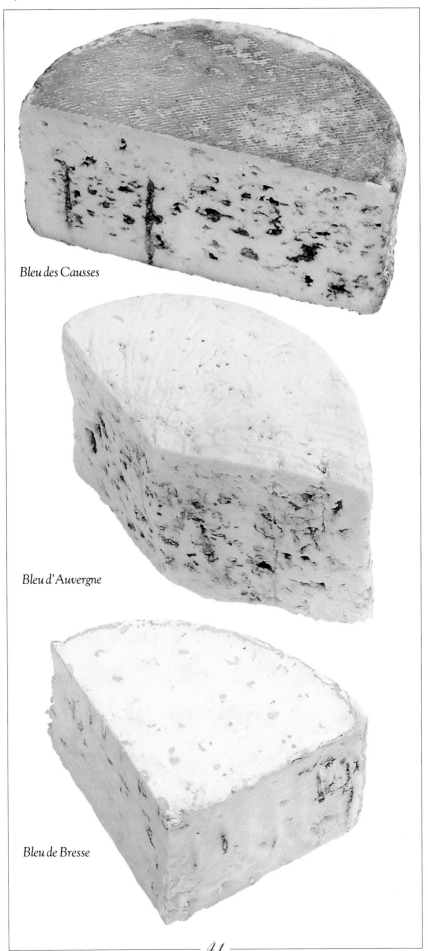

Bleu des Causses

Bleu d'Auvergne

Bleu de Bresse

Bleu de Sassenage

BLEU DE SASSENAGE

A traditional, French, cows' milk cheese made in the Dauphine. It has a 45% fat content and a smooth natural rind. It takes three months to cure and reaches peak condition in summer and autumn when made from pasture milk. Similar in size to Bleu de Gex, it has a supple, fine-grained texture and lightly coloured, well-distributed veins. The flavour is slightly sharp and bitter.

BLUE BRIE

A commercially-created soft blue cheese which is something of a phenomenon, as it has a bloomy white rind which is free of blue moulds and therefore almost certainly sprayed on. Ripened cows' milk is innoculated with *penicillium* moulds, then pierced to encourage development. The predominantly white paste resembles ordinary brie in texture but is slightly thicker. In flavour, blue brie is mild and rather bland, making it popular with hesitant blue eaters.

BLUE CHESHIRE

The original English Blue Cheshire came about by accident when mould developed in standard Cheshire cheeses. These rarities were known as Green Fades. Today, the moulds are deliberately intro-duced and consequently the cheeses are much faster developing with a better distribution of veins. A full-fat, lightly-pressed cheese (too much pressure would inhibit the flow of oxygen to the veins) with a thick, craggy, natural crust, blue Cheshire has a superb balance of strength and richness with nutty background notes. The veins are a dark greeny-blue, contrasting with the deep yellow, annatto-dyed paste. It is a considerably stronger cheese than ordinary Cheshire.

Two closely related cheeses are **Trinity,** which is harder in texture and deeper in colour, and **Shropshire Blue** which has a more rugged looking rind.

BLUE VINNY

Once a popular English cheese made from partially skimmed milk, Blue Vinny disappeared from the market in 1982, though inferior Stiltons often tried to pass themselves off as such. Genuine Dorset Vinny, however, had to be made and ripened in the tack room of a stable to attract the bacteria necessary for its unique character. One Dorset farm is now producing the real thing again, but supplies of the 4.5 kg (10 lb) tubby, drum-shaped cheese are limited. It is a firm cheese with strong dark veining, which can taste rather dull.

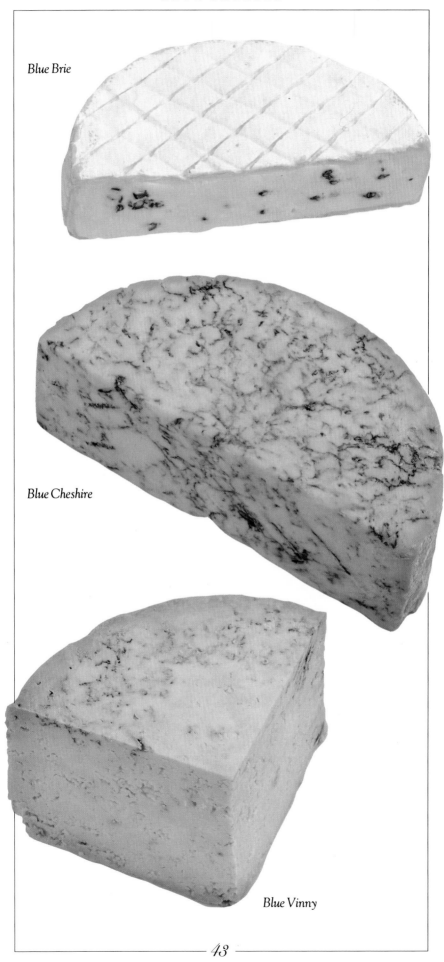

Blue Brie

Blue Cheshire

Blue Vinny

Blue Wensleydale

BLUE WENSLEYDALE

A semi-hard, cows' milk English cheese which is similar to Stilton but less creamy and crumbly. This cheese has been made since the 12th century, though not in its present form until the beginning of this century: prior to that it was almost entirely blue. During the second world war, local production ceased, to be re-established later in the neighbouring county of Derbyshire. Now it is once again made in the Wensleydale area.

CAMBAZOLA

A blue Brie-type German cheese of fairly recent invention. Like blue Brie, it is entirely factory-made with synthetically produced moulds and a washing-powder white, sprayed-on bloomy rind. The paste is creamy white and soft with delicate blue-green veining. It is made in dinner plate sized wheels with a portion-marked foil wrapper.

CASHEL BLUE

A modern Irish cheese which combines the sweetness of a Gorgonzola with the pungency of a raw milk Stilton and the creaminess of a Roquefort. It is, however, loosely based on the recipe for a German blue cheese, Edelpizkase. Made in 1.5 kg (3 lb) foil-wrapped drums from unpasteurized cows' milk, it ripens in around two months. When mature, Cashel Blue has a thin supple rind, creamy pink-tinged paste (the pink is due to endemic local moulds) and well-distributed blue-grey veins.

DANISH BLUE

This cheese was invented by Marius Boel, a Danish cheese-maker, early this century. He introduced a bread mould to a high fat cheese and so created Danish Blue, now so popular that it is widely imitated worldwide. It has a stark, white paste with aggressive blue-black veining and a strong, bitter, salty flavour. It is made from pasteurized, homogenized cows' milk and is foil-wrapped.

DORSET BLUE

A full-fat Stilton-type English cheese once widely made in the Dorset area, but production now is confined to a single farm in Sturminster Newton. Made from unpasteurized cows' milk, its scarcity value is its chief interest.

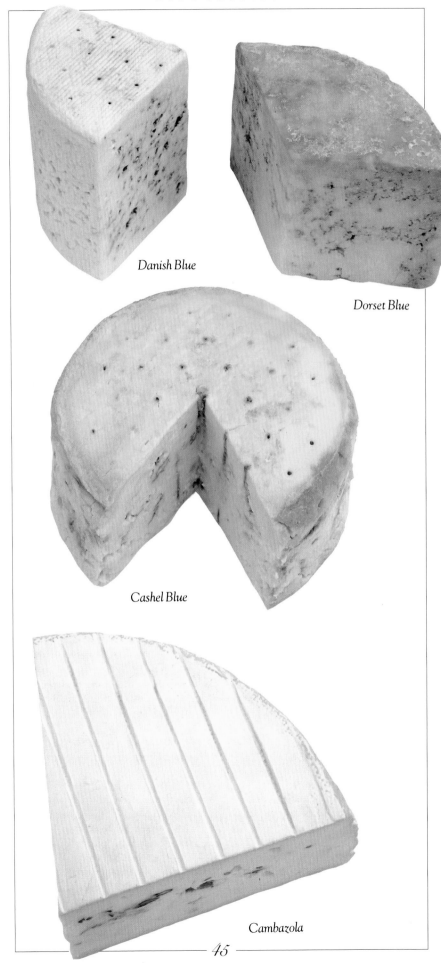

Danish Blue

Dorset Blue

Cashel Blue

Cambazola

Fourme d'Ambert

FOURME D'AMBERT
This cheese takes its name from the Latin noun *forma*, which describes its cylindrical shape. A full-fat, cows' milk cheese, it is one of the rare French blues to have a crust. It is a very old-established cheese, known to have been made since the 7th century, and is as highly regarded by gourmets as Roquefort. Fourme is made by farms and small dairies and at its best is extremely creamy, nutty and full-bodied. Though quite supple, it should have plenty of 'give'. Its best seasons are summer and autumn.

FOURME DE MONTBRISON
An almost identical cheese to Fourme D'Ambert in all respects, including its natural, dark grey rind. The main difference is origin: this cheese comes from the Forez province. Its prime seasons are also summer and autumn, when it is made from the best quality milk.

GORGONZOLA
This popular, well-known Italian cheese holds the distinction of being the oldest named cheese in the world: its first recorded mention was in AD 879. The town of Gorgonzola, after which it is named, was an established resting point for cattle on their annual winter drive from the alpine pastures to the stalls and this abundance of milk, together with the mould-rich local caves, conspired to produce excellent cheese. Unlike most blues, where even veining is desirable, Gorgonzola should have a greater concentration of moulds towards the centre of the cheese. This is because two days' curds with conflicting acidities and consequently poor homogeneity are used. Only one company now makes Gorgonzola according to traditional methods; the commercially-made cheeses are invariably *dolce* (soft, sweet and like a Dolcelatte), not *piccante* (firm, heavily-blued with a strong, spicy flavour) as the original.

HARBOURNE BLUE
A limited production goats' milk English blue from the same maker as Beenleigh Blue that is quite superb. Named after the Devonshire river close to where it is matured in a disused wine vat buried in the side of a valley, it has a firm yet creamy texture and full, goaty flavour. It is made in 2.5 kg (5 lb), foil-wrapped drums and is best kept refrigerated until just before serving.

LANARK BLUE
A recently established, hard ewes' milk cheese which is made according to a traditional Roquefort-type recipe in Scotland. Like all ewes' milk cheeses, it is seasonal, but sometimes the development of young cheese is artificially arrested by chilling to ensure year round availability. These adulterated cheeses should be avoided.

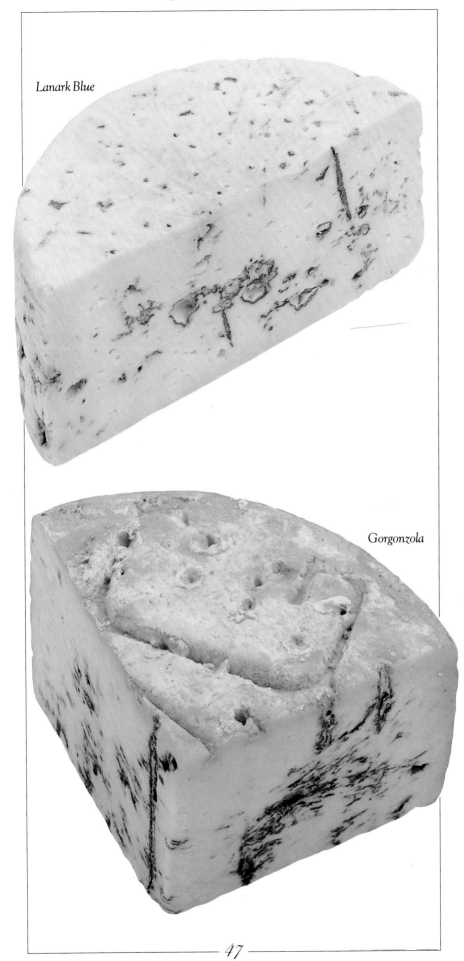

Lanark Blue

Gorgonzola

LYMESWOLD

A soft English cheese first made in Somerset in 1982 to utilize surplus milk. It is based on the German Bavaria Blau recipe. Like this cheese, it is lightly streaked with blue and has an artificially promoted bloomy white rind. When young, the cheese is quite supple with a mild delicate flavour which intensifies as it matures, developing distinct, tangy notes. Made in a Brie-shaped disc, it is usually foil-wrapped. Despite extensive launch promotion, it has never really made a serious assault on the home market.

MYCELLA

A semi-soft Danish cheese which is pale yellow in colour with a deep green veining. The name is derived from the *mycelium* mould which lends the cheese its character. It has a pale brown crust and full Gorgonzola-like flavour.

ROQUEFORT

The most famous of all French blue cheeses, Roquefort's sublime nature fully deserves such renown. A very ancient cheese, it dates back to the time of the Gauls and was even mentioned by Pliny the elder in his Historia Naturalis. It was also a favourite of the Emperor Charlemagne, Charles VI and several popes.

According to experts, it owes its popularity not to the creamy, concentrated, unpasteurized ewes' milk from which it is made, nor to the *penicillium roqueforti* moulds (also present in many other cheeses), but rather to the enormous limestone caves (called *cabanes)* in which it is matured. During the three months that the cheeses are cured there, natural spores circulate freely and aid their development.

Smooth, firm and buttery textured, Roquefort has a strong, well-rounded flavour and a faint mould aroma. Roquefort is protected by strict government legislation so tends to be of consistently good quality. However, like all the ewes' milk cheeses, it should be avoided during the spring months when it is almost certain to have been unnaturally preserved. The foil wrapper which protects its skin should be removed only immediately before serving to prevent dehydration.

SAINGORLON

A French-made blue cheese which is an exact imitation of Gorgonzola. Acceptable if the real thing proves difficult to come by.

STILTON

If Roquefort is the King of French blues, then Stilton has a justifiable claim to the English crown. As befits royalty, it has a bodyguard in the form of an association which protects its trade mark. Although it originated in the Cambridgeshire town of the same name, now the only counties permitted to produce the *bona fide* article are Leicestershire, Nottinghamshire and Derbyshire. All manufacturers use whole, British cows' milk but only one, the Colston Bassett Dairy in Nottingham, uses unpasteurized milk.

A semi-hard cheese, Stilton is unpressed – hence its velvety, smooth texture – and has a thick, natural crust. The paste should be cream coloured, never white, and spread with greeny-blue veins. Young Stilton has a mild, sharp quality which, when aged, gives way to a pronounced, full flavour. Stilton should never be scooped or macerated in port: both practices do the cheese a great dis-service.

WHARFEDALE BLUE

A hard blue cheese from Yorkshire made from goats' milk. It is square in shape, weighs around 1.5-2 kg (3-4 lb) and is finished with yellow wax to prevent moisture loss. Fairly mild when young, it has a powerful, well-developed flavour when fully mature. Wharfedale Blue is made in small quantities only.

WHITE STILTON

Included here because if kept long enough, white Stilton will eventually blue. It is firmer and milder than blue Stilton and a perfectly acceptable and refreshing alternative.

Roquefort

Stilton

White Stilton

Lymeswold

Uncooked Pressed Cheeses

This group encompasses a vast number of cheeses of greatly varying characters and textures. This variation is largely dependent upon the manufacturing process. In cheeses where the curd is transferred directly from ripening vat to weighted mould, the texture will be softer than in those whose curds are cut and milled to achieve a firm density. Obviously, this also affects the overall development of the cheese. All uncooked pressed cheeses have a natural rind, but in some cases this is scraped away and the cheese finished with wax to cut down on moisture loss. On those cheeses not treated thus, the marks of the cloth which lined the mould will often be clearly visible. Curing, which again varies enormously in duration, generally takes place in cool humid cellars.

ASIAGO

There are two varieties of this Italian mountain cheese from the Veneto. One, **Asiago de Allievo**, made in the mountain region of Vezzana from the unskimmed milk of cows grazed on summer pasture, is a seasonal hard cheese, at its best from mid-autumn to spring. The other, **Asiago Pressato**, is made from skimmed cows' milk and is an extremely close-textured, grainy cheese. When young it may be eaten sliced, but as it matures it becomes more suitable for grating. Made in medium-sized wheels weighing between 8-11.75 kg (17½-26½ lb), it has a yellowy-beige paste and glossy, rich straw-coloured rind.

BEAUMONT

Made in the Savoie province of France, Beaumont is distinguished by its tri-coloured red, white and blue paper wrapper. Made chiefly from unpasteurized cows' milk, it is at its best when made from spring and summer pasture milk. A whole cheese weighs around 1.75 kg (3½ lb) and has a regular, white-golden rind, close texture and supple, springy feel. Its creamy mild flavour is widely appreciated.

CAERPHILLY

This cheese takes its name from the Welsh village of Caerphilly. The creamy white, moist and crumbly cheese has a mild, salty flavour and a floury-white hard rind. It is said to be one of the most easily digested cheeses. Caerphilly closely resembles Wensleydale and like that cheese, it is particularly good served as a dessert, partnered with tart fruit pies.

CANTAL

A giant of a cheese from the Auvergne province of France, cantal is made in drums approximately 46 cm (18 in) in diameter and 41 cm (16 in) high, each weighing between 36-45 kg (80-100 lb). Sometimes called Salers, it is made from full fat cows' milk and has a grey rind and cream paste. Excellent as a table cheese, it is also valuable as a flavouring for cooked dishes such as soups, sauces and gratins. A semi-hard cheese, it comes in varying strengths from mild to strong. It is most versatile when creamy-tasting with background notes of nuts.

CASTLE HILL

A Cheddar-type cheese with a smooth firm texture and clean, sharp lingering flavour. Formerly a kitchen cheese (ie, domestically made) it is now commercially produced in limited quantities. Two sizes are available: a 4.5 kg (10 lb) flat wheel and a 2.5 kg (5 lb) drum-shaped cheese. The smaller of the two is probably a better buy as it presses more satisfactorily, resulting in a closer texture, and matures more quickly. Made from unpasteurized cows' milk, Castle Hill is also suitable for vegetarians as it is made using non-animal rennet.

Castle Hill

Cantal

Asiago

Caerphilly

Cheddar

CHEDDAR

Indisputably England's most famous cheese, Cheddar is also its most widely imitated: Australia, Canada, Denmark and New Zealand all make their own equivalents using the original 'cheddaring' technique devised in its native Somerset. This process involves cutting the curd repeatedly until a hot iron draws out a continuous elastic string when inserted. Once this is achieved, the whey is drained off and the curd cut with knives and stacked. This reduces its acidity levels and so brakes the development of the cheese.

Nowadays, most Cheddar is made in blocks from pasteurized cows' milk, rather than from unpasteurized milk in the traditional drum-shape, and is sadly lacking in character. The best Cheddar is matured for a minimum of nine months, though often it is sold much younger than this. It should be neither crumbly nor rubbery in texture but smooth and firm. Colour can be anything from pale ivory, through cream to annatto-dyed red. Mild, medium or mature, it is certainly one of the most versatile cheeses on the market.

CHESHIRE

The English Cheshire recipe has been exported worldwide, yet no other country has succeeded in reproducing the clean, acidic, nutty notes of this cheese, which are balanced by a meaty mellowness and moist, friable texture. A cows' milk cheese, made from both pasteurized and unpasteurized milk, Cheshire has a high acidity level which lends it its characteristically, flaky open texture. Now made almost entirely by factories, the only traditional Cheshire is made in Shropshire. Non-block Cheshires are made in large drums weighing 36 kg (80 lb) or more and have a smooth, even rind verging on waxiness.

COTHERSTONE

One of the Dales' cheeses, Cotherstone (pronounced Cutherstone) was created by French monks during the time of William the Conqueror. It is made with a mixture of milk from Channel Island and Friesland cattle and because of its high fat content, matures quickly. Left much longer than three to four weeks, it has a tendency to blue naturally. Made in the form of millstones, each 2.5 kg (5 lb) semi-soft cheese has a natural crust which varies in colour from pale apricot to deep, pink-gold, depending on the season, degree of ripeness and the surface moulds. The paste within is creamy in texture and pale gold in colour.

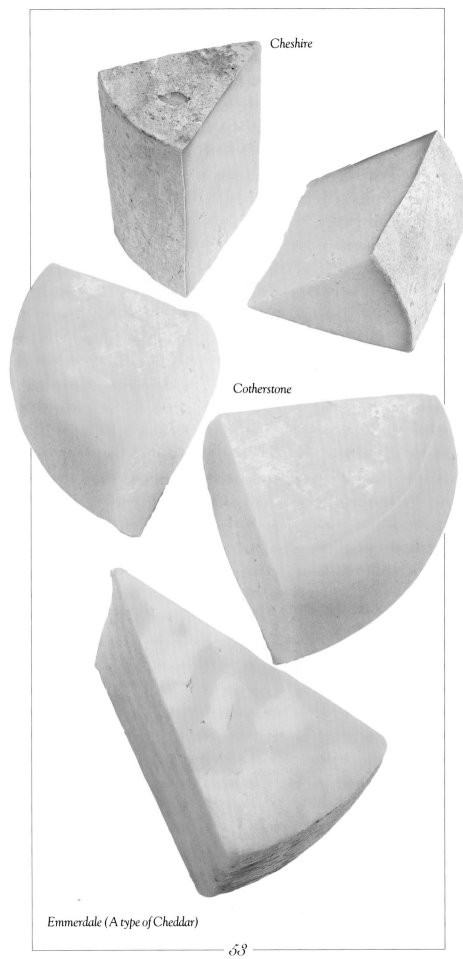

Cheshire

Cotherstone

Emmerdale (A type of Cheddar)

DERBY

One of the oldest-established of all British cheeses, Derby has affinities with both Cheddar and Cheshire but is somewhat softer in texture and more delicate in flavour than either. In its original form, this cows' milk cheese was made in drums about 38 cm (15 in) in diameter and 13 cm (5 in) deep, with a natural, wax-finished rind. Nowadays it is almost entirely made in rindless blocks and is relatively obscure. Better known is Sage Derby, a herb-flavoured variant. This cheese has a waxy close texture with a fresh, green-marbled appearance and pronounced sage flavour, achieved by adding a liquid extract of the herb to the curds before moulding and pressing.

EDAM

Dutch Edam is almost as well-known as Cheddar. It originates from the town of the same name. Similar to Gouda in taste, it is distinguished by being made from partly skimmed pasteurized cows' milk with a fat content of 30-40%. It is manufactured entirely by factories in elongated 1.5-2 kg (3-4 lb) balls finished with red or yellow wax and has a smooth, supple waxy texture and sharp, slightly acidic flavour. It is much favoured by slimmers as it combines all the versatility of a hard cheese with the virtues of a reduced calorie content. It is also available flavoured with cumin seeds or red peppers, in which case it has a brown-tinted rind.

EXMOOR

A Jersey milk, English Devonshire cheese of limited production which owes its origins to Wensleydale. Although made all the year round, winter cheeses are generally superior to those made during the summer months, being softer and creamier with a refreshingly sour-sweet flavour. Summer cheeses have a firm, flaky texture and a deep, buttercup-yellow paste. The cheese has a fairly thin natural crust, varying in colour from golden brown to light grey.

FONTAL

A native of both France and Italy, Fontal is a full-fat cows' milk cheese made exclusively by commercial dairies. It is consistent in quality throughout the year and comes in the form of a flat cylindrical wheel about 41 cm (16 in) in diameter and 11 kg (24 lb) in weight. The cheese has a smooth, even, brushed rind, homogenenous ivory-white paste and mild fruity flavour. A good cooking cheese, it is ideal in fondues and toasted cheese dishes.

FONTINA

Related to Fontal and similar in most respects, this long-established Piedmontese cheese was the gentry's choice as early as the 13th century. Unlike Fontal, however, it is made solely by alpine chalets in the Piedmont region of Italy and has a more obvious bouquet. Its ivory-yellow paste differs from Fontal, in that it is peppered with tiny holes. Fontina is a highly regarded Italian cheese, with a mild, yet distinctive flavour and a supple texture. Mature cheeses, with their firmer, drier texture, are particularly suitable for use as a condiment, grated.

GLOUCESTER (SINGLE)

This is the original Gloucester cheese – softer, milder and faster maturing than the ubiquitous Double Gloucester – with a fresh, light flavour. The cheese dates back to the 8th century when it was held in low esteem as a thin cheese, meaning one which is made from lower fat morning milk, or hay cheese, a reference to the fact that it was considered fit for consumption only by the harvest labourers. Genuine single Gloucester is made purely from the milk of Old Gloucester cows – not the higher yielding Friesans favoured by commercial dairies. Only one maker, Charles Martell, produces the genuine article and his name has in recent years becomes synonymous with this cheese. Single Gloucester is best eaten at about ten weeks of age and benefits from the sap-filled zest of spring pasture milk.

Exmoor

Edam

Fontal

Single Gloucester

Derby

Fontina

GLOUCESTER (DOUBLE)

A traditional English farmhouse cheese with a pale orange paste (it is coloured with annatto) and a flavour which ranges from mellow and creamy to quite strong, depending upon the maturity of the cheese. The best Double Gloucesters are made from unpasteurized, full-cream, summer-pasture cows' milk. The adjective double refers to the fact that the traditional recipe for the cheese relied upon the milk from both morning and evening milkings. Such refinements are, however, largely ignored by the commercial dairies who make the block Double Gloucester which accounts for the bulk of the market. This cheese is slower to mature than Single Gloucester.

GOUDA

One of Holland's foremost cheeses, Gouda has been marketed for more than two hundred years. Most of the cheese that is exported is young cheese, no more than six weeks old. This is quite salty and dull in flavour, and can be recognized by its yellow-wax coating. Mature Gouda is an altogether superior cheese with a stronger, more pronounced flavour and a black wax coating. The average weight of this flat wheel-shaped cheese is approximately 4 kg (9 lb), though both smaller and larger cheeses are available. Made from unpasteurized cows' milk, Gouda has a high butter-fat content which contributes to its succulent creamy flavour.

HURSTONE

A descendant of the original Dunlop, which was a Scottish sweet or full-fat milk cheese. Like Dunlop, Hurstone is made from Jersey cows' milk which, with its high fat content, makes this a rich creamy cheese. It is lightly pressed with a smooth close texture and comes in 2.5 kg (5 lb) and 4.5 kg (10 lb) drums. It reaches its peak at around three months old and its best season is autumn, when mature cheeses are redolent with the flavours of summer meadow herbs and flowers. Summer cheeses are also much deeper in colour, owing to a high concentration of carotene in the milk. Although only limited quantities of this cheese are available, it does belong to the great tradition of British cheese-making, which is currently enjoying a revival.

LANCASHIRE

Another traditional British farmhouse cheese which is now largely made in block form by commercial dairies. Authentic Lancashire has a very unusual and labour-intensive manufacturing process. Milk from both evening and morning milkings is ripened and the resulting curd hand broken, pressed and cut repeatedly within a short period. It is then combined with curd from the previous day, salted and milled before being transferred to moulds and matured. Finished cheeses are waxed to prevent moisture loss. This rather long-winded procedure results in a cheese which is moist and flaky with an attractive, acidic flavour. As the cheese matures it becomes smoother and silkier, almost buttery, and correspondingly sweeter. Try it the way Lancastrians eat it – with slabs of fruit cake.

LEICESTER

Traditionally the name Leicester was synonymous with what we now know as Red Leicester: White Leicester came about as a result of a ban on food colourings during the second world war and remained after this was lifted. A fairly hard-textured cheese, with an edible natural rind, it is made in commercial blocks or 9 and 18 kg (20 and 40 lb) drum shapes, noteworthy because at 51 cm (20 in) across, they have the largest diameter of any English cheese. The flavour of Leicester is difficult to define when young, but as the cheese matures it develops a distinct nuttiness all of its own, which is complemented by its harder texture.

Double Gloucester

Leicester

Gouda

Lancashire

Leyden

LEYDEN
A Dutch cheese known as Leidsche Kaas in its homeland, this waxed rind, pressed cheese is made from full-fat cows' milk and flavoured with caraway seeds. It is subjected to a two-pronged cure: first in humid cellars, then in a dry atmosphere. Made in the form of a flat cylinder with slightly convex sides, it has a firm supple texture and mild flavour enlivened by the caraway. A clove-flavoured version of this cheese is also produced.

MIMOLETTE
Another Dutch cheese made from full-fat unpasteurized cows' milk. It is semi-soft in texture with a rustic-looking even rind, dense, orange-coloured paste (this is artificially coloured) and pleasant nutty flavour. Each cheese weighs around 2.5 kg (5 lb) and is shaped like a flattened ball. There is also a French version of this cheese, made in Flanders, which is practically identical.

PRESENT
A Dutch, Gouda-style cheese which can be made from pasteurized or unpasteurized milk. It is similar to young Gouda in both taste and texture, being mild with a faint nutty background and firm supple consistency.

TOMME DE SAVOIE
Perhaps the best known of all the extended Tomme family, this deliciously mild cows' milk cheese has a fat content of only 20-40%. It has a firm, smooth yellow paste and hard, powdery natural crust which is predominantly grey but flecked with mimosa and red pigments.

Individual cheeses weigh around 2-3 kg (4-7 lb) and are cured for approximately two months: one month in cool humid cellars, followed by a month in a warmer environment to encourage the flavoursome surface moulds. In texture Tomme de Savoie is silky smooth and supple. This cheese is at its best during the winter.

WENSLEYDALE
Cheese was first made in the Wensleydale region during the Norman invasion, when French monks from the Roquefort region were brought over to Britain to practise their cheese-making skills. Originally, like the cheeses after which they were fashioned, they were made from ewes' milk, but are now made from cows' milk exclusively by commercial dairies. A mild lightly salted cheese, Wensleydale has a crumbly, creamy-white paste and refreshing flavour. It is delicious served with fruit or even fruit pies, as is the local custom.

Tomme de Savoie

Mimolette

Wensleydale

Hard, Cooked Cheeses

Not necessarily always hard, but certainly always firm, these cheeses are said to be 'cooked' because the curd, after being broken up, is heated in the whey before being wrapped in cloth and transferred to the moulds. The curd is then pressed down as far as possible to eliminate the maximum amount of moisture. This process subjects the cheese to a special fermentation which, during the course of ripening in warm cellars, makes it swell and develop apertures or holes. They are generally large cheeses, sometimes weighing more than 45 kg (100 lb) with natural brushed and washed rinds.

APPENZELL
Also known as Bloderkäse, this Swiss mountain cheese is made in alpine chalets from the milk of cows grazed high in the alpine pastures. Smaller than many cheeses of this type (each wheel weighs a mere 5-7 kg (11-15 lb) it is very firm in texture and its paste is dotted with perfectly formed pea-sized holes. Its rind is quite smooth. During its three to six month curing period, the cheese may be washed with herb- and spice-infused white wine or cider. Appenzell has a pronounced fruity flavour and is ideal for cooking purposes.

BEAUFORT
Widely acknowledged to be the finest of the Gruyères, Beaufort is made in the Haute Savoie and Savoie *départements* of France, the milk from whose meadows lends the finished cheese a magnificent flowery-sweet, fruity flavour with a slight salty tang. An *appellation d'origine contrôlée* cheese, this seal of approval guarantees that the cheese has been made and matured in the Savoie mountains for a minimum of four months. This is important, as the mountain caves are liberally endowed with *bacterium linens* which help to form the cheese's crust and so retain the moisture of the creamy smooth paste. Made in enormous wheels, a whole Beaufort weighs between 41-59 kg (90-130 lb). The cheese is in quite short supply.

BITTO
From Lombardy in Italy, this rustic cheese has been produced in the same way for the past ten centuries. The cheese is made from a mixture of cows' and goats' milk. Fresh Bitto is ready in two months. The young cheese is pale and creamy but as it matures it develops a strong, aromatic flavour which closely resembles that of Parmesan.

COMTÉ
Another French member of the Gruyère family, its patronymic is actually Gruyère de Comté. Made from cows' milk in the moutainous Franche-Comté region since the 13th century, prime specimens have round marble-shaped holes. Comté has a stronger flavour than an Emmental: fruity and salty with a marked bouquet. Its rind is tough and darkly coloured, enclosing a yellowish paste. Pleasant when eaten alone, it is also wonderful as an ingredient in a wide variety of cooked dishes: fondues, gratins, soufflés and sauces suggest themselves immediately.

EMMENTAL
A Swiss mountain cheese made from cows' milk and copied by other countries, notably France. The firm, thick, oily, golden paste has evenly distributed olive-shaped holes and a soft fruity flavour. Made in wheels which can weigh as much as 100 kg (220 lb), it is identifiable by the label of origin on the side of each cheese. According to French cheese expert Pierre Androüet, its size came about because of the necessity to store up dairy products over the alpine winters. Like Comté, Emmental is good as a table cheese and as an ingredient: in salads, canapés or sprinkled over soups and vegetables, or in cooked dishes.

Emmental

Comté

Beaufort

Appenzell

FJORDLAND

A Norwegian cheese made from partially skimmed cows' milk. It has a pale smooth paste and unevenly distributed large round holes. It bears a passing resemblance to Emmental.

GRUYÈRE

First and foremost a Swiss national, Gruyère is now widely copied by other countries, including France and the United States. It is named after the village of its origin in the canton of Fribourg, where it is still made in small, mountain fruiteries. The cheese has a pale yellow, firm but friable paste, which is sparsely scattered with pea-sized holes. It has a rather sweet, fruity flavour, significant aroma and coarse reddish rind in which fine slits, known as *becs,* may be discerned. Wonderful both as a table cheese or a recipe ingredient.

HERRGARDSOST

One of the most popular of all Swedish cheeses, Herrgardsost has been produced there since the turn of the century. A cows' milk cheese, its paste is medium firm and pliable with a sweet nutty flavour and a similar size and distribution of apertures to Gruyère. The cheese is salted in brine then, about two weeks later, wax-finished. This makes it an extremely good keeper – it will show no sign of deterioration for at least a year. Like Gruyère, Comté and Emmental, this cheese melts easily when heated and consequently is suitable for use in cooked dishes.

JARLSBERG

An Emmental-type cheese from Norway with a pronounced, nutty flavour. It is made from full-cream cows' milk and has a golden yellow paste, slight sweetness and even distribution of large apertures. Once considerably cheaper than Emmental, its popularity has dispensed with its price advantage.

PARMESAN

Parmesan is the popular name of the best known of the *grana* family of Italian cheeses. Its correct name is Parmigiano Reggiano. This costly but rewarding cheese is made from skimmed cows' milk mixed with rennet and cooked for about 30 minutes, until the curds separate. The cheese comes in vast, shiny brown drums, weighing as much as 40 kg (88 lb), with the name stamped vertically all over the side. If the cheese bears no such identification, it is not the genuine article, although other similar cheeses can be quite acceptable. Strict legislation controls its manufacture: it must be made between 15th April and 11th November.

A good Parmesan has a pale yellow paste with pin-head holes and a closely grained texture. When young and mild it is suitable for use as a table cheese. A whole Parmesan will keep for years, improving all the while. A cheese marked *vecchio* will have been matured for two years, one marked *stravecchio* for three years, and a *stravecchione* is an extra mature, four-year-old cheese. Young Parmesan will readily become hard, granular and grateable if stored in the refrigerator.

Parmesan is a basic ingredient of Italian cooking for the very good reason that it does not form threads as it melts. Grated, it is added to soups, sprinkled over pasta and rice, and used as a seasoning in vegetable and polenta dishes. It is also good on salads.

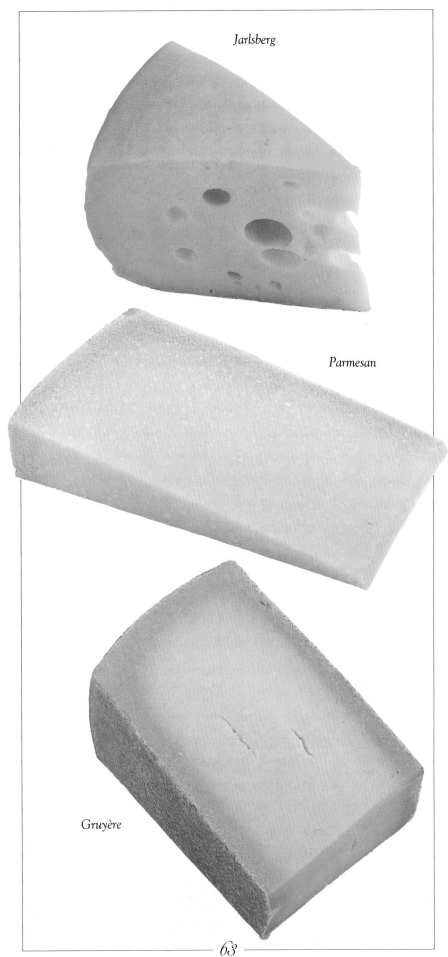

Jarlsberg

Parmesan

Gruyère

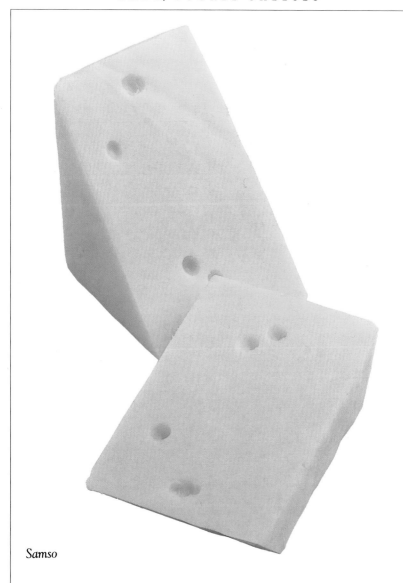

Samso

SAANEN
A very hard Swedish cheese with a brittle, deep yellow, hole-pitted paste. It is similar to Parmesan, having almost indefinite keeping qualities and, grated, may be used in much the same way.

SAMSO
An all-purpose, Danish, semi-hard, full-cream cows' milk cheese with a mild, sweet, nutty flavour when young. Mature cheeses are stronger and more pungent. The interior is pale yellow, with holes the size of cherries. As well as being an attractive dessert cheese, it lends itself well to cooking, particularly fondue and gratin-type dishes.

SAPSAGO
Made in Switzerland, Sapsago has many names, including Schabzieger and green cheese. It is virtually fat-less, being made from the reheated whey of skimmed cows' milk. A semi-hard cheese, it has a cylinder-like shape tapering towards the tip. Sapsago's flavour is strong and spicy and its texture is extremely hard, making it suitable only for grating. The unusual pale green colour of this cheese is achieved by the addition of clover and powdered fenugreek. It is sold foil-wrapped, or powdered in cartons.

SBRINZ
Also known as *fromage à raper* (grating cheese), this Swiss full-fat cows' milk cheese has a dark yellow rind, dense yellow interior and brittle, hard texture. Seldom used as a table cheese, it is, like Parmesan, almost always used grated as a seasoning or recipe ingredient and was probably created to do away with the need to import Parmesan.

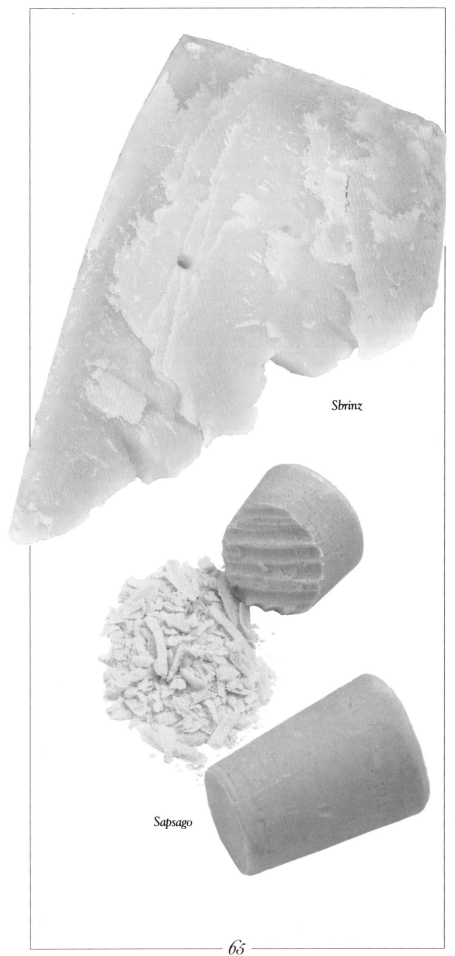

Sbrinz

Sapsago

Goats' Milk Cheeses

Goats' milk cheeses run a whole gamut of flavours, textures and types. Originally made in areas of poor pasture where only these hardy beasts could survive, they have become something of a cult and this has resulted in a large upsurge of numbers.

Continental goats' cheeses are invariably soft, depending on the way in which the curd is treated. They are not, strictly speaking, cured, but rather drained and allowed to dry out: for this reason it is perfectly possible to mature a fresh cheese at home provided suitable conditions exist.

Mature continental goats' cheeses have either a natural blue-mould rind, or a thick, white, artificially generated *penicillium* rind. Sometimes they are coated in charcoal ash *(cendre)*, flavoured with herbs or wrapped in leaves.

While many producers of British goats' cheeses follow the continental lead, an increasing number base their recipes on traditional British hard cheeses, lending them an altogether different character. Goats' milk cheeses can be mild, subtle, lactic, sharp, brittle or just plain goaty – therefore they should always be approached with an open mind.

Because the EEC has largely devoted itself to the cause of cows' milk pasteurization, goats' milk cheeses are invariably made from raw milk which results in a better quality, more interesting cheese.

BANON

A mild soft cheese from Provence which is sometimes also made with ewes' or cows' milk. The goats' milk variety is at its best from late spring to early autumn. The cheese has a fat content of 45% and a natural rind attractively presented in a raffia-tied wrapper of chestnut leaves which have been marinated in *eau de vie*. These 'parcels' are left to ferment in terracotta jars for a period of two weeks to two months, according to the desired degree of strength. They have a mild, lactic, nutty flavour, firm supple texture, sticky rind and faint dairy odour. An alternative version is made, known as **Banon au Pebre d'Ai**, which is flavoured with summer savory.

BOUGON

This cheese from Poitou in France is similar in taste and texture to Bucheron but differs in appearance as it is moulded into a flat, cylindrical shape. A soft cheese with a bloomy rind, it ripens in about two weeks and weighs about 280 g (9 oz). It is usually boxed before sale.

BUCHERON

A French cheese sometimes known as Buche de Chèvre. The cheese has a thick, fluted white rind and is moulded in the shape of a log.

CASTLE ASHBY

A medium strength, semi-soft English cheese made in Northampton. It is matured for just ten days, during which time it is coated with ash to form a soft, grey crust. The cheese is pyramid shaped and weighs about 375 g (12 oz).

CHABICHOU

A small, truncated cone-shaped cheese from Poitou, the stronghold of French goats' cheese production. A farmhouse cheese, Chabichou has a thin, blue, reddish-tinged rind, pronounced goat smell and strong, sharp flavour. It takes three weeks to mature.

HALOUMI

A soft to semi-soft Cypriot cheese which is salty, yet quite mild. It is generally served toasted and can be quite rubbery.

Bucheron

Banon

Chabichou

Haloumi

Bougon

Mendip Goat

MENDIP GOAT

A bulbous, thick-rinded cheese which is part of the British cheese-making revival, Mendip Goat is made in the west country from the milk of Anglo-Nubian and British Sannens goats. It has a sweet, complex flavour which really comes into its own when made from spring pasture milk. At that time of the year it has, according to one of Britain's foremost chefs, the nose of truffles. One noteworthy feature of this cheese is the lattice indentations on its crust; these are caused by the plastic colanders in which it is moulded. Mendip Goat takes approximately five months to mature and is available in limited quantities only.

MONTRACHET

A tall, cylindrical cheese from Burgundy, Montrachet is practically rindless. It is usually ripened in vine or chestnut leaves which should be removed before serving. Other versions are ash-covered, or coated with chopped herbs. Individual cheeses weigh about 90 g (3 oz) and take about ten days to ripen. Supple in consistency, this cheese has a faintly discernible 'goaty' smell and mild creamy flavour.

MOTHAIS

Also known as Mothe-Sainte-Heray, this commercially-made cheese comes plain or with a *cendré* coating. The former are disc-shaped, the latter pyramid-shaped: both weigh approximately 250 g (8 oz). Tender rather than soft in texture, they are quite robustly flavoured. From the Poitou province of France.

RIBBLESDALE

A lightly pressed, wax-finished English cheese made in north Yorkshire. It has a moist, semi-soft texture, and delicate, mild, lightly salted flavour. The cheese varies from season to season with the variations in protein and fat content of the milk. Winter cheeses are softer and creamier than their crumblier, summer and autumn counterparts. An oak-smoked version is also made.

SAINT-CHRISTOPHE

At its best from early spring until mid-autumn, Saint-Christophe comes from the Tourangeau region of France, where goats' milk cheeses are thought to have been first introduced by the Saracens back in the Middle Ages. A log *chèvre* with a natural rind, Saint-Christophe is modelled on the original log *chèvre*, Sainte-Maure. It has a deliciously creamy, succulent softness and perfectly balanced flavour when made from summer pasture milk. Saint-Christophe has the rustic finishing touch of a straw running through its paste to facilitate lifting during ripening.

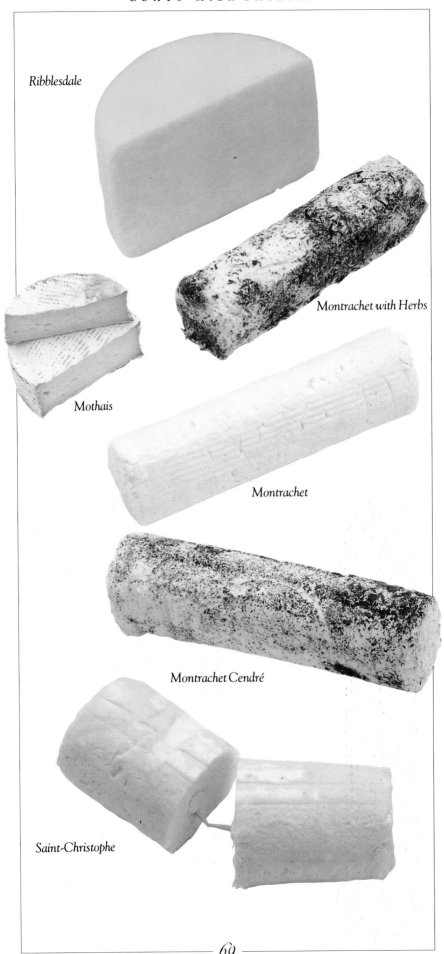

Ribblesdale

Montrachet with Herbs

Mothais

Montrachet

Montrachet Cendré

Saint-Christophe

Sainte-Maure

SAINTE-MAURE

Also known as Chèvre Long, this log-shaped cheese from Touraine was originally produced solely on farms but is now made chiefly in factories. It has a bloomy, artificial rind, strong mould aroma and full goat flavour. Packaged in paper, in deference to its forebears, it is sometimes made with a straw running through its centre. It has a firm but yielding texture which can develop graininess if improperly kept. It is cured in cool, dry cellars for approximately one month.

SATTERLEIGH

A Devonshire goats' cheese made on much the same lines as a Cheddar, Satterleigh is a firm, subtly-flavoured cheese which is at its best from late spring until early winter. A hard, pressed cheese, it is made in 2 kg (4 lb) drums and matured for approximately four months. As a young cheese it is white, but as it matures it develops a creamy complexion. Unlike many goats' cheeses, it is very stable and hard to mis-handle.

TOMME DE L'ARDÈCHE MERIDIONALE

A traditional *chèvre* from the heart of the Ardèche, this is one of the oldest established and most consistently successful of all the *chèvre* family. Made in the form of flattish discs, each weighing about 410 g (13 oz), these cheeses mature in about five weeks. Tomme de l'Ardèche Meridionale has a gently undulating crust imprinted with the marks of the straw mats on which it is matured and delicately flecked with blue moulds. It has a delightful fresh flavour, light texture and complex bouquet. Resist the impulse to remove its rind before eating, as many experts believe that the greatest depth of flavour is concentrated there.

TYMSBORO

A soft mild cheese which is ready to eat after just two to three weeks maturation. This English cheese is made from unpasteurized goats' milk in the heart of Shakespeare country. It is either round or pyramid-shaped. Tymsboro is mould-ripened and therefore has a white, downy rind, generally flecked with blue.

VALENÇAY

Both creamery and farm versions of this cheese are made in the Poitou region. The creamery type has an artificially promoted bloomy rind, while the farm cheese is natural and charcoal-dusted. Both are an attractive pyramid shape and weigh approximately 315 g (10 oz). The farm cheese is seasonal, at its best from spring to autumn when it has a deep, blue skin, firm yet tender consistency, delicate goat and mould aroma and mild, nutty flavour. The creamery version is available all year round (off season it is made from frozen curd). This cheese is contrastingly firm and supple with an intense nose and undistinguished, salty flavour.

Valençay

Tymsboro

Tomme de L'Ardèche Meridionale

Ewes' Milk Cheeses

Creamy, white ewes' milk is a great deal more concentrated than that of either cows or goats. It has much higher levels of both fat and casein (an important substance for the formation of curd). It is ideally suited to both soft and hard cheese-making processes and the resulting cheeses are rich and flavoursome regardless of their strength.

The chief drawback lies with the faster maturing cheeses: because ewes' lactate only between spring and autumn, they are unavailable during the winter. Some producers attempt to bridge the gap by freezing curd to be matured during the colder months, but this is largely unsuccessful as cheeses made from frozen curd never develop as well as their fresh curd counterparts. It is worth noting, however, that finished cheeses may be frozen without detriment, provided they are eaten on the day of thawing.

These cheeses deserve attention on their own merits but are also invaluable for those who suffer allergies to cows' milk cheeses yet find goats' milk cheeses too strong.

AMOU

A French, uncooked, pressed cheese from Gascony, made exclusively by farms. It has a natural golden-coloured rind whose neat appearance is the result of frequent washings and oilings during its two to six month curing period. Depending on age, its texture may be firm and resilient or hard and crumbly; its flavour too, progresses from mild to quite sharp. Mature cheeses are better grated and used like Parmesan than eaten as they are. Amou is made in the shape of a thick disc and each cheese weighs approximately 4.5 kg (10 lb).

ANNOT

Sometimes referred to by its more formal title, Tomme d'Annot, goats' milk may sometimes be substituted for ewes' in its manufacture when supplies are short. Made by mountain farms in the Comte de Nice province of France, it is a disc-shaped, uncooked pressed cheese with a smooth pale rind. It has a mild, nutty flavour, supple texture and faint sheep aroma. Cured for about two months, it is at its best throughout the summer.

BARAC

A hard, Scottish cheese made in much the same way as the English Dales' cheeses, Barac is acknowledged by experts to be one of the best British ewes' cheeses in existence. It has a superb balance of sweetness and acidity and a soft, crumbly consistency when young. If matured for longer than the normal six to seven months, the flavour gains depth and the texture smoothness; colour, too, deepens from pure white to cream. Only limited quantities of this excellent cheese are available.

FIORE SARDO

Also called Pecorino Sardo, this lightly-pressed cheese from Sardinia has a natural white to yellow oiled rind, and fresh, nutty flavour which develops sharp, salt notes as the cheese matures. Soft as a young cheese, it hardens with age when it is best used grated, as a seasoning.

LARUNS

A semi-cooked pressed cheese from the Basque country, this cheese is made in the form of a flattened loaf about 30.5 cm (12 in) in diameter, 9 cm (3½ in) deep and weighing about 5.5 kg (12 lb). It has a smooth, thin natural crust which varies in colour between straw-yellow and ochre. It is cured in humid cellars for two to six months, according to whether it is destined for table or pot. After two months, it is tender yet supple with a mild, nutty flavour. Older cheeses are hard and brittle with a very strong, sharp flavour. It is essentially a domestic cheese.

Barac

Fiore Sardo

Sheviock

NIOLO

A soft, farmhouse cheese from Corsica with a natural, lightly brine-washed rind. It is made in a rounded square shape, imprinted with the marks of the basket in which it is moulded, and each cheese weighs about 725 g (1¼ lb). Its rind has a smooth, clean, greyish-white appearance and smells strongly of sheep. In mature cheeses, the paste is firm, buttery and sharply flavoured with a full bouquet. Fresh, unripened cheeses are mild, creamy and oily-textured.

PECORINO ROMANO

A very ancient Italian, cooked, pressed cheese made in dairies around Rome. It has a somewhat lower fat content than most related cheese – only 36%. Made in medium-sized cylindrical wheels, each weighing between 6-12 kg (13-26 lb), it has a natural white to dark yellow rind (some cheeses are oiled using olive oil dregs tinted with ochre) and white to pale yellow paste. A densely textured cheese with a hint of smoke about its aroma, Pecorino Romano is aged for a minimum of eight months and is extremely strong. Younger cheeses are suitable for table but mature specimens are best treated as aged Parmesans.

PECORINO SICILIANO

Also called Canestrato, after the baskets in which the curd is drained, this Sicilian cheese is uncooked and pressed and also differs from its Roman cousin in that it has a slightly higher fat content – usually more than 40%. Similar in size to Pecorino Romano, it is matured for half as long yet attains equal strength of character. It is something of an acquired taste, being fiercely sharp and almost rancid. It has a natural white to yellow oiled rind and a dense, white paste.

SHEVIOCK

A relatively new British cheese made with milk from British milk sheep and marinated in cider from its native Cornwall. It is made to a Cheddar recipe and has a smooth moist texture and subtle refreshing flavour. The drum-shaped cheese weighs about 2 kg (4 lb), has a good, natural crust and is made in limited amounts only.

Pecorino Romano

Pecorino Siciliano

Spenwood

SPENWOOD
Another newly-established British ewes' milk cheese of limited production and consistently high quality. It is made in wheels of approximately 2.5 kg (5 lb) and has either a natural rind the colour of Portland stone or a waxed finish. In common with most ewes' milk cheeses, Spenwood is at its best when made from spring pasture milk and its flavour benefits from its five months maturation. At this age it has a smooth, supple, slightly grainy texture and a mild flavour which is reminiscent of barley.

SARTENO
An uncooked, pressed cheese from Corsica with a filmy, pale yellow natural rind, Sarteno may be made from goats' milk or a combination of both ewes' and goats' milk. Made in the form of a flattened sphere of about 13 cm (5 in) in diameter and 10 cm (4 in) in depth, each cheese weighs between 1-1.25 kg (2-2½ lb) and is matured for three months in dry cellar conditions. At this age it has a firm but not brittle texture, subtley penetrating aroma and strong sharp flavour. It is named after the principal market town in the south west of the island and is thought to have been manufactured in this region since Roman times. Sarteno is best eaten young as a dessert cheese but more mature specimens may successfully be used grated, as a seasoning or garnish in much the same way as Parmesan.

TOMME DE BRACH
A soft ewes' milk cheese from the Massif Central region of France which is made almost entirely on farms. It is at best during spring and summer. Tomme de Brach has a smooth, natural rind and somewhat oily consistency. Cured in dry cellars for between two and three months, each small, drum-shaped cheese weighs about 750 g (1½ lb) and is 10 cm (4 in) in diameter. It has a fairly strong flavour and definite sheep aroma. The term 'tomme' is simply a French dialect word for cheese; it does not refer to a specific cheese grouping.

TOMME DE CARMARGUE
Sometimes known as Tomme Arlesienne, this soft, fresh cheese originates from Provence. It is made by small dairies and is at its best during spring and winter. Mild and creamy, it is flavoured with ground thyme and bay leaves. It has no rind, but a filmy pale ivory skin to which a bay leaf is banded. Tomme de Carmargue has a mild, creamy flavour, with a suggestion of herbs. It is usually moulded in small squares of about 6 cm (2½ in), and allowed to drain for 1 week. It can, if desired, be aged quite successfully. Like most tommes, it is difficult to find outside France.

Venaco

TOMME DE VALDEBLORE

An uncooked, pressed ewes' milk cheese from the Comté de Nice province of France, Tomme de Valdeblore is a mountain cheese which is sadly becoming increasingly scarce. Cured in dry cellars, with occasional bursts of humidity, for anything from three to six months, it has distinctive characteristics according to its age: young cheeses have a pinkish-grey rind, tender but supple consistency, mild, creamy lactic taste and are virtually without aroma; mature cheeses have a grey-brown rind, hard texture (which retains some give), sharp flavour and pronounced sheep aroma. Locally, older cheeses are considered superior; elsewhere younger cheeses are preferred. Made in flat cylinders of 9 kg (20 lb) or more, this cheese is closely related to Tomme d'Annot.

VENACO

A soft, Corsican mountain cheese which may also be made from goats' milk. It has a natural rind which is generally scraped away leaving a greyish-white surface. The cheese is matured in humid rock caves for three to four months and has a firm oily texture, powerful fermented smell and pronounced, sharp sheep flavour. Venaco can be eaten as it is or, as Corsicans enjoy it, mashed and marinated in robust red wine.

Soft Cheeses with Natural Rind

This category of cheeses falls somewhere between those with bloomy rinds and those with washed rinds. On the whole, they develop neither the softness of the first, nor the pungency of the latter. The ripening of such cheeses is double-edged: both from the interior to the rim and from the crust to the centre. In a good, even-textured cheese, these two processes will have kept pace with each other. A number of cheeses in this group are coated with wood ash (cendre) during curing; this not only looks attractive but improves the flavour and keeping qualities.

BARBEREY

A Champenois cheese which is also known as Fromage de Troyes or Troyen Cendré, Barberey is made by small dairies using skimmed cows' milk and has a fat content of a mere 20-30%. Cured in wood ash for about a month, the cheese has a subtle musty aroma and rather sharp flavour. It is made in small discs, weighing about 250 g (9 oz). Barbery is at its best during spring and autumn.

FRINAULT

A full-fat cows' milk cheese from Orléans in France, which is at its best when made from summer and autumn pasture milk. Named after its creator, it has a delicately coloured, bluish rind, tender-soft texture and full flavour. It takes just three weeks to come of age because of its diminutive size: each whole, thin disc-shaped cheese weighs only 125 g (4 oz). A cendré version is also made. Frinault is closely related to Olivet Bleu.

GUÉRET

A farmhouse cheese from the Marche province of France which also goes by the name of Creusois or Coupi. It is made from cows' milk which is almost completely skimmed to give a fat content as low as 10%. Guéret is an irregular disc-shaped cheese, about 13 cm (5 in) in diameter and 3.5 cm (1½ in) deep. It is ripened in sealed terracotta pots for up to six months, depending on conditions. The resulting cheese has an ultra-smooth, sticky rind, pronounced smell and quite mild flavour. In appearance, the paste is translucent. It is used both as a dessert cheese and grated, sprinkled over local dishes.

HEILTZ LE MAURUPT

A rustic, ash-coated cheese made from partially skimmed cows' milk which is also known as Cendré d'Argonnes. Production is centred in the Champagne region of France and geared towards the hay and grape harvests when it is served to farm labourers. Dry-cured for two to three months, the cheese has a firm but yielding consistency, insignificant aroma and strong, spicy flavour. Whole cheeses are Camembert-sized but lighter, weighing only 315-375 g (10-12 oz). Try serving this cheese instead of the usual Cheddar as the basis of a deliciously different ploughman's lunch.

MIGNOT

This full-fat cows' milk cheese from Normandy reaches prime condition during the autumn and winter. It is made entirely on farms and matured in humid cellars for one month. Firm and fruity with lots of bouquet, it has a red, oily natural rind and pale ivory paste. It comes in discs about 13 cm (5 in) in diameter and 3.5 cm (1½ in) deep.

NOYERS LE VAL

Another harvest cheese which is made by farms in the Champagne region of France to sustain labourers during grape-picking. The cheese is made from semi-skimmed cows' milk with a fat content of 30-35% and is cured in ash in dry cellars for between two and three months. It is firm and quite supple in texture and though it has no aroma worth speaking of, this is more than compensated for by its strong, spicy soapy flavour. In appearance Noyers le Val is attractively rustic: an irregularly-shaped disc which is liberally coated with ashes. Whole cheeses are about 13 cm (5 in) in diameter, weighing 375 g (12 oz).

Frinault

OLIVET BLEU

A traditional, dairy-made cheese from the Orléanais province of France. It is made from whole cows' milk and has a natural, blue, quite bloomy rind. It is cured in local chalk caves for approximately one month and sold *au naturel,* or wrapped in paper or plane tree leaves. Its season extends from spring to the end of autumn, during which time it has a smooth, straw-yellow paste, even, rich, supple texture and mild fruity flavour. It is made in the form of small, flat discs weighing about 345 g (11 oz). A *cendré* version is also produced, which takes rather longer to reach maturity.

OLIVET CENDRÉ

Olivet Bleu's ash ripened relative, Olivet Cendré also hails from the Orléanais province of France. Like Olivet Bleu, it is made in traditional dairies from cows' milk but has a slightly lower fat content of around 40%. Because of its slower maturation period – three months as opposed to one – its season extends into the winter months. The two cheeses are practically identical in size, about 13 cm (5 in) in diameter, though quite different in appearance and flavour. Olivet Cendré's distinctive grey ash coating contains a much more savoury, firmer, full-bodied cheese. (Illustrated on page 80.)

Olivet Cendré

PANNES CENDRÉ
This is the same type of cheese and from the same area as Olivet Cendré, the chief difference being that Pannes Cendré is made from skimmed cows' milk. A thick, handsomely-shaped cheese, it has a supple texture, natural mould and strong flavour with soapy background notes.

RIGOTTE DE CONDRIEU
A full-fat cows' milk Lyonnaise cheese made entirely by small dairies and available all the year round. It has an annatto-tinted natural rind, so thin as to be barely discernible. Because of its minute size (whole cheeses are 3.5 cm (1½ in) in diameter and depth), it takes only two weeks to mature in dry conditions. It is quite a firm textured cheese with an indistinct aroma and mild, occasionally lactic flavour.

RIGOTTE DE PELUSSIN
A traditional farmhouse cheese from the Auvergne, unusual in that it is made with a mixture of cows' and goats' milk. Rigotte de Pelussin is made in the form of a squat cone, a mere 2.5 cm (1 in) in height and weighing only 90-100 g (3-3½ oz). Because of its tiny size, it ripens in a mere three weeks in dry cellar conditions, during which time it develops a delicate, blue-tinged rind and an appealing mild, nutty flavour. It should be firm in texture, never dry. Rigotte de Pelussin may also be made purely from goats' milk.

SAINT-MARCELLIN
According to French legend, this is the cheese that once sustained Louis XI after an ordeal involving a bear in the Forest of Lenta, close to where it is made. In those days, though, the cheese would almost certainly have been made from goats' milk; this was later combined with cows' milk and today it is made exclusively from the latter by farms and small dairies. A small, soft, supple cheese, it has a thin, apricot-coloured rind which is flecked with delicate, blue-grey moulds, a faint, lactic nose and refreshingly sharp flavour. It is ripened first in humid caves, then later in ventilated drying rooms for a total of one month. Saint-Marcellin is muffin-sized, about 8 cm (3 in) in diameter, and weighs only about 100 g (3½ oz).

Saint-Marcellin

Rigotte de Condrieu

Processed Cheeses

Just as commercially-produced pasteurized cheeses can never compete with raw milk farm cheeses for their subtle nuances of flavour and amazing range of textures, processed cheeses are at a distinct disadvantage, being manufactured according to scientific formulae rather than traditional recipes. Nonetheless, provided they are chosen with care some can be a welcome addition to the cheeseboard and they do have the virtue of keeping well, being of a more stable nature. A word of warning though: while it may be acceptable to serve a Roulé or a Tomme au Raisin, it is unforgiveable to offer a square of processed plastic in place of proper Cheddar!

AUSTRIAN SMOKED CHEESE

A medium-fat, sausage-shaped cheese with a firm, rubbery texture which is lightly smoked. It is made from cows' milk and sold in wax-finished portions.

BEL PAESE

An Italian, foil-wrapped soft cheese with a buttery, spreadable texture which is often sold in individual portions. It has a mild, fruity flavour and appealing, lactic aroma and is ideal for sandwiches.

HUNTSMAN

This is the brand name of one of the many layered cheeses on the market. Huntsman is an English cheese made by a dairy in Melton Mowbray, Leicestershire, and consists of a layer of Stilton sandwiched between two layers of Double Gloucester cheese. Numerous variations on this theme exist but unfortunately, and without exception, they look rather better than they taste.

ORANGERULLE

A full-fat soft, fresh, tube-shaped cheese which is flavoured with Grand Marnier and rolled in hazelnuts. It is rather rich, but quite pleasant as a dessert.

ROULÉ

A soft, fresh cheese not dissimilar in texture to a *chèvre*, which is now widely available. The cheese is spread with either herbs and garlic or fruit and formed like a Swiss roll. It is sold pre-sliced and looks quite attractive.

TOMME AU NOIX

A soft bland cheese with an ivory white paste whose surface is studded with walnuts. The actual cheese was originally made in Savoie and ripened in caves but production has now shifted entirely to factories. The nuts are quite a pleasant foil to the smoothness and bland flavour of the cheese.

TOMME AU RAISIN

Sometimes also called Fromage au Raisin, like Tomme au Noix this cheese originated in the Savoie province of France where it was ripened in a mixture of grape skins, pulp and pips. Nowadays, factory-produced cheeses are rolled in black grape pips after manufacture and consequently lend little to the flavour of the white paste. The cheese is mild and quite fruity, with a chewy texture.

WINDSOR RED

A Cheddar-style cheese which is flavoured and coloured with elderberry wine; the Irish do the same thing with Guinness. Red Windsor has a crumbly texture and a flavour similar to mild Cheddar.

Tomme au Raisin

Bel Paese

Austrian Smoked

Tomme au Noix

Windsor Red

Huntsman

Roulé

Orangerulle

Danish Dip

155 ml (5 fl oz/⅔ cup) single (light) cream

155 ml (5 fl oz/⅔ cup) dry white wine

2 egg yolks

125 g (4 oz) Danish blue cheese, coarsely crumbled

2 teaspoons finely chopped dill weed

TO GARNISH:

sprigs of dill

TO SERVE:

selection of raw vegetables, including julienne strips of carrot, red and yellow pepper, and courgette (zucchini), celery sticks, cauliflower flowerets, and blanched asparagus spears

In a bowl, blend together cream and wine; immediately beat in egg yolks. Stir in cheese. Pour into the top section of a double boiler or a bowl set over a pan one-quarter filled with barely simmering water. Cook for a few minutes, stirring constantly, until thick and smooth. Remove from heat and stir in dill weed. Leave to cool. Pour into a serving dish and chill until required.

To serve, place the dish of cheese dip in the centre of a serving platter, garnish with dill and surround with prepared vegetables.

Makes 315 ml (10 fl oz/1¼ cups).

Horseradish Dip

125 g (4 oz/½ cup) fromage frais
4 teaspoons grated horseradish
¼ teaspoon black pepper
¼ teaspoon garlic salt

In a bowl, blend together all the ingredients. Leave in a cool place for 3-4 hours for the flavours to develop, then pour into a serving dish. Accompany with pretzels, poppadums and cheese straws (see note).

Makes 155 ml (5 fl oz/⅔ cup).

Note: To make cheese straws, roll out some ready-made puff pastry on a lightly floured surface. Using a sharp knife, cut into finger-size rectangles. Brush with beaten egg and sprinkle with grated cheese and sesame, poppy or caraway seeds.

Put the pastry rectangles on a dampened baking sheet and bake in a preheated oven 200C (400F/Gas 6) for about 10 minutes, until well risen and golden brown. Transfer the cheese straws to a wire rack to cool.

White Stilton & Leek Soup

3 leeks, about 375 g (12 oz) total, weight, thinly sliced

1 small potato, diced

785 ml (25 fl oz/3 cups) homemade chicken stock

125 g (4 oz) white Stilton cheese, crumbled

pepper to taste

2 tablespoons single (light) cream

TO GARNISH:

sprigs of parsley, or a few reserved leek rings

Put leeks into a large saucepan with potato and stock and cook for about 20 minutes or until vegetables are soft.

Purée vegetables and stock in a blender or food processor until smooth. Return soup to pan and add Stilton. Heat gently, stirring constantly, until cheese melts; season with pepper.

Divide soup between individual bowls and spoon over a little cream. Create a feathered effect using a cocktail stick or a small skewer. Garnish each portion with parsley sprigs, or leek rings (see note).

Serves 4-6.

Note: It is important to use a good homemade stock as a commercial stock cube is not suitable for this recipe.

To garnish with leek rings it is important to blanch the leek first, otherwise the flavour will be too strong: add to boiling water, leave for 2 minutes, drain, then refresh under cold running water.

Cheese & Artichoke Chowder

2 tablespoons butter
1 small onion, sliced
500 g (1 lb) Jerusalem artichokes, sliced into water with 1 tablespoon lemon juice added
250 g (8 oz) carrots, sliced
5 teaspoons plain flour
625 ml (20 fl oz/2½ cups) chicken or vegetable stock
315 ml (10 fl oz/1¼ cups) milk
250 g (8 oz) Gruyère cheese, grated
½ teaspoon dry mustard
salt and pepper, to taste
JULIENNE GARNISH:
1 artichoke
1 carrot
1 leek
a little chervil

In a large saucepan, melt butter, add onion and cook for 1 minute, stirring constantly. Drain artichokes; add to pan with carrots. Cook for 2 minutes. Add flour, then gradually add stock. Cover and simmer for 20 minutes.

Meanwhile, prepare julienne garnish. Cut artichoke, carrot and green part of the leek into julienne strips. Blanch in boiling water for 1 minute; refresh in cold water and set aside.

Blend soup in a food processor or blender until smooth. Add milk, cheese and seasonings and blend again. Pour into a clean pan and reheat gently; do not boil.

Pour into individual soup bowls and garnish with the prepared vegetables and chervil leaves.

Serves 4.

Avocado with Mascarpone

4 avocados, ripe but firm, halved

3 tablespoons freshly squeezed lemon juice

125 g (4 oz) mascarpone cheese

1-2 teaspoons French mustard

1 clove garlic, crushed

few drops tabasco

salt and pepper, to taste

TO GARNISH:

30 g (1 oz/¼ cup) flaked almonds

sprigs of parsley

chive flowers (optional)

Carefully scoop out avocado flesh using a teaspoon, making sure skins remain whole; set skins aside. Roughly chop the flesh, put into a bowl and sprinkle with 1 tablespoon of the lemon juice, to prevent discolouration.

In a separate bowl, blend cheese with mustard to taste, garlic and remaining lemon juice. Season with tabasco, salt and pepper. Add chopped avocado and mix in carefully. Pile into avocado shells and chill for about 20 minutes.

Garnish with almonds, parsley, and chive flowers if available, and serve in individual dishes.

Serves 8.

Note: This tasty dish can alternatively be served, with French bread, as a light lunch for 4 people.

Chaource Mousse & Chive Sauce

4 large crisp lettuce leaves

1 teaspoon butter

30 g (1 oz/¼ cup) chopped button mushrooms

1 stick celery, very finely chopped

1 shallot, chopped

125 g (4 oz) chaource cheese, white rind removed, crumbled

3 tablespoons fromage frais

155 ml (5 fl oz/⅔ cup) cold chicken or vegetable stock

2½ teaspoons gelatine, dissolved in 2 tablespoons stock

2 teaspoons snipped chives

2 teaspoons chopped parsley

pinch of dry mustard

salt and pepper, to taste

SAUCE:

1 egg white

1 tablespoon crème fraîche

3 teaspoons snipped chives

GARNISH:

a few lettuce leaves

carrot julienne

Plunge lettuce leaves into boiling water, then immediately plunge into cold water. Drain on absorbent kitchen paper. Use to line 4 oiled ramekins.

In a small saucepan, melt butter, add mushrooms, celery and shallot and cook for 1 minute. Remove from heat and set aside.

Put cheese, fromage frais and stock into a food processor or blender and blend until smooth. Slowly add dissolved gelatine and blend again. Stir in cooked vegetables, herbs and seasonings.

Spoon the mixture into prepared ramekins, putting the leaves over the filling to enclose it. Chill until set.

Make sauce a few minutes before serving: whisk egg white until soft peaks form, fold into crème fraîche and add chives.

Turn the mousses onto 4 individual plates and spoon over a little sauce. Garnish with lettuce leaves and carrot. Serve with melba toast.

Serves 4.

Grilled Chèvre with Walnuts

4 x 90 g (3 oz) slices chèvre
½ curly endive, broken into pieces
few radicchio leaves, broken into pieces
1 head chicory, cut diagonally into 1 cm (½ in) slices
handful of rocket leaves
30 g (1 oz/¼ cup) chopped walnuts
DRESSING:
3 tablespoons walnut oil
2 teaspoons white wine vinegar
½ teaspoon clear honey
salt and pepper, to taste

Place chèvre on a piece of oiled foil in a grill pan.

Put endive, radicchio, chicory and rocket leaves in a bowl.

Put all dressing ingredients in a screw-top jar and shake vigorously until emulsified. Pour over salad, toss thoroughly and arrange on 4 individual plates.

Put the chèvre under a preheated moderate grill for 1-2 minutes, until melting; place 1 slice on each salad.

Sprinkle with walnuts and serve immediately.

Serves 4.

Note: Chèvre may also be bought in rolls, which have a 3.5 cm (1½ in) diameter. Buy 2 x 200 g (6½ oz) rolls and cut them into 12 slices. Serve 3 grilled slices per person.

Baked Haloumi in Vine Leaves

250 g (8 oz) haloumi cheese
16-20 vine leaves, packed in brine
SAUCE:
3 teaspoons cornflour
315 ml (10 fl oz/1¼ cups) tomato juice
2 teaspoons lemon juice
¼ teaspoon black pepper
¼ teaspoon sugar
¼ teaspoon ground bay leaves
1 teaspoon shredded basil leaves
TO GARNISH:
basil leaves

Pat haloumi dry with absorbent kitchen paper and cut into sixteen to twenty 1 cm (½ in) slices; divide into small bars and set aside.

Soak vine leaves in a large bowl of cold water for 30 minutes to remove brine. Drain, then plunge one at a time into a large pan of boiling water and blanch for 2 minutes. Drain and pat dry with absorbent kitchen paper.

Preheat oven to 230C (450F/ Gas 8). Brush a shallow ovenproof dish liberally with oil.

Place a piece of cheese near stalk end of each vine leaf; fold in sides and roll up to form small packets. Pack stuffed vine leaves closely together in a single layer in prepared dish. Brush generously with olive oil and cook in the oven for 15-20 minutes, until crisp.

To make sauce, blend cornflour with a little of the tomato juice, stir in remaining juice, then place all sauce ingredients in a heavy-based saucepan over medium heat. Whisk constantly until thickened.

Serve stuffed vine leaves hot, on a pool of sauce, garnished with basil leaves.

Serves 8-10.

Note: This dish can alternatively be served as a main course for 4-5 accompanied with rice.

Deep-fried Cambazola

250 g (8 oz) firm cambazola (or similar blue brie-type cheese)

60 g (2 oz/½ cup) plain flour

salt and pepper, to taste

2 eggs

60 g (2 oz/½ cup) dry breadcrumbs

oil for deep-frying

TO GARNISH:

4 Victoria plums, stoned and sliced

TO SERVE:

8 tablespoons Chinese plum sauce

Using a small sharp knife, remove white rind and cut cheese into 2 cm (¾ in) cubes.

Season flour with salt and pepper. Beat eggs in one bowl; put breadcrumbs in another.

Dip cheese cubes in seasoned flour, coating each piece thoroughly; shake off excess. Next dip in beaten egg, then breadcrumbs to coat thoroughly, firmly patting them into place with a table knife. Chill for 20 minutes.

One-third fill a deep-fryer with vegetable oil and heat to 182C/360F. Using a slotted spoon, carefully lower cheese cubes one at a time into hot oil; do not overfill pan – cook cubes in batches. Deep-fry for 3-4 minutes, until golden brown; remove with slotted spoon and drain on absorbent kitchen paper. Serve immediately on warmed plates, as the melted cheese oozes out on standing. Garnish with sliced plum and a little Chinese plum sauce.

Serves 4-5.

Note: Chinese plum sauce is available from specialist Chinese stores, some supermarkets and delicatessens.

Roquefort Purses

125 g (4 oz) filo pastry

15 g (½ oz) butter, melted

45 g (1½ oz) Roquefort cheese, cut into 12 cubes

12 chives

oil for deep-frying

TO GARNISH:

chives

Cut pastry into twelve 8 cm (3 in) squares. Pile on top of each other and cover with a cloth to prevent drying out.

Brush one square with butter; place another on top to make an 8-pointed star, then brush with butter. Put a cheese cube in the centre. Bring up edges of pastry to cover cheese and pinch together into a money bag shape – the butter will help pastry to stick together. Tie a chive round top. Repeat with remaining pastry, cheese and chives.

Heat oil in a deep-fryer until a cube of bread turns brown in 1 minute. Place 'purses' in basket and deep-fry for 1 minute, until crisp and golden brown. Drain thoroughly on absorbent kitchen paper.

Garnish with chives and serve immediately on individual plates.

Serves 4-6.

Note: Serve 2 or 3 of these little purses as a pretty starter. Alternatively, they make an excellent addition to a buffet and are ideal to serve with drinks.

Blue Brie & Broccoli Flan

PASTRY:

280 g (9 oz/2¼ cups) plain flour

pinch of salt

140 g (4½ oz) butter, at room temperature

1 egg yolk

3-4 tablespoons cold water

FILLING:

185-250 g (6-8 oz) broccoli

185 g (6 oz) Lymeswold or blue Brie white rind removed

2 tablespoons single (light) cream

3 eggs, beaten

2 tablespoons chopped parsley

salt and pepper, to taste

To make pastry, sift flour and salt into a bowl; add butter. Using 2 table knives, cut butter into flour until pea-sized and well coated with flour. Beat egg yolk with 3 tablespoons water; add to bowl and mix to form a soft dough; add more water if necessary. Form pastry into a ball and flatten slightly into a round shape with floured hands. Wrap in plastic wrap and chill for 15 minutes.

On a lightly floured surface, roll out pastry and use to line a 23 cm (9 in) flan dish. Prick base with a fork; chill for 10 minutes.

Preheat oven to 190C (375F/ Gas 5).

To make filling, cook broccoli in boiling salted water for 5-6 minutes. Drain, rinse in cold water, drain thoroughly, then chop roughly. Set aside.

Break cheese into pieces and put in the top of a double boiler or a bowl set over a pan of barely simmering water. Heat gently until melted. Remove from heat. Beat together cream and eggs, then blend into melted cheese. Stir in parsley and season lightly with salt and pepper.

Put broccoli in flan case, pour over cheese mixture and bake in the oven for 30-40 minutes or until lightly browned and set. Serve warm, with a salad.

Serves 6-8.

Asparagus & Salmon Quiches

PASTRY:

90 g (3 oz/¾ cup) plain flour

45 g (1½ oz/3 tablespoons) oatmeal

90 g (3 oz) butter

about 2 tablespoons cold water

FILLING:

½ Camembert

125 g (4 oz) smoked salmon

16 asparagus tips, blanched

1 egg

155 ml (5 fl oz/⅔ cup) single (light) cream

salt and pepper, to taste

cayenne pepper

TO GARNISH:

sprigs of parsley

Preheat oven to 200 C (400F/ Gas 6).

To make pastry, place flour, oatmeal and butter in a food processor and blend for 45 seconds. Add water and blend for 15 seconds or until pastry binds together. Divide pastry into 4, roll out on a floured surface and use to line four 11 cm (4½ in) individual flan tins. Chill while preparing filling.

Cut Camembert into 8 segments; cut each segment in half horizontally. Cut salmon into 16 small strips; roll up. Place 4 segments of Camembert in each flan case, rind side down, and arrange salmon rolls and asparagus tips on top.

Beat egg and cream together; season with salt, pepper and a little cayenne. Pour into flan cases and bake in the oven for 25 minutes, until set firm.

Serve warm, garnished with parsley, with a mixed salad.

Serves 4.

Note: If you do not have a food processor, make pastry by rubbing in method, mixing oatmeal with flour.

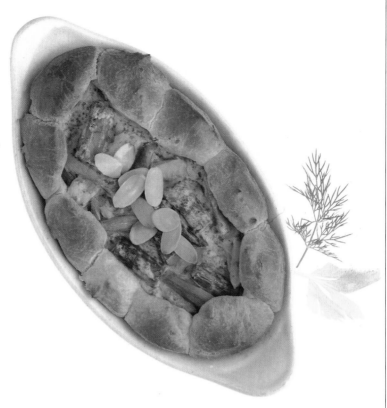

Smoked Trout Gougère

CHOUX PASTRY:

60 g (2 oz) butter
155 ml (5 fl oz/²⁄₃ cup) water
75 g (2½ oz/²⁄₃ cup) plain flour, sifted
2 eggs plus 1 yolk, beaten
pepper to taste
90 g (3 oz) Austrian smoked or Cheddar cheese, grated

FILLING:

30 g (1 oz) butter
185 g (6 oz) celery hearts, thinly sliced
250 g (8 oz) asparagus, cut into 2.5 cm (1 in) pieces
3 teaspoons plain flour
155 ml (5 fl oz/²⁄₃ cup) single (light) cream
3 smoked trout
6 teaspoons chopped parsley
6 teaspoons lemon juice

TO GARNISH:

30 g (1 oz/¼ cup) flaked almonds, toasted

Preheat oven to 200 C (400F/Gas 6). Butter a large shallow baking dish or 4 individual ovenproof dishes.

First, prepare filling. In a large saucepan, melt butter; sauté the vegetables for 1 minute; stir in flour. Remove from heat and gradually add cream; return to heat and bring to boil, stirring, until thickened.

Remove skin and bones from trout; flake flesh into large pieces. Add to pan with parsley and lemon juice; remove from heat.

To make pastry, in a medium saucepan, melt butter in water over gentle heat; bring to boil. Remove from heat and tip in flour all at once; beat with a wooden spoon until dough is smooth and leaves side of pan. Beat in egg a little at a time until dough is smooth and shiny. Season with pepper and stir in 50 g (2 oz) cheese.

Spoon choux mixture evenly around edge of prepared dish(es). Fill centre with fish mixture; sprinkle with remaining cheese. Bake in the oven for 30 minutes (20 minutes for individual gougères) until well risen and golden. Sprinkle with almonds and serve immediately.

Serves 4.

Pizza Quattro Formaggi

DOUGH:

250 g (8 oz/2 cups) plain flour
30 g (1 oz) butter or margarine
½ teaspoon salt
¼ teaspoon sugar
1 packet 'easy blend' dried yeast
about 140 ml (4½ fl oz/½ cup) warm water

FILLING:

15 g (½ oz) butter or margarine
1 small onion, thinly sliced
400 g (14 oz) can tomatoes
1 teaspoon dried oregano
black pepper to taste

TOPPING:

60 g (2 oz) mozzarella cheese, thinly sliced
30 g (1 oz) Gorgonzola cheese, crumbled
45 g (1½ oz) fontina cheese, sliced
45 g (1½ oz) bel paese cheese, sliced
50 g (2 oz) can anchovy fillets, drained, or 4 lean bacon slices, cut into strips
8-12 pitted black or stuffed green olives

Sift flour into a mixing bowl; rub in butter or margarine; stir in salt, sugar and yeast. Mix in sufficient warm water to form a soft dough; knead until no longer sticky. Cover bowl loosely with plastic wrap and leave to rise in a warm place for about 1½-2 hours, until doubled in size.

Meanwhile, prepare filling. In a large frying pan, melt butter or margarine; sauté onion until soft. Stir in tomatoes with their juice, oregano and pepper. Mash thoroughly and cook for about 10 minutes, stirring frequently, until thick.

Grease a large baking sheet. Preheat oven to 200 C (400F/Gas 6).

In centre of baking sheet, press out dough to a 20.5 cm (8 in) round. Cover with prepared filling to within 1 cm (½ in) of edge. Cover each quarter of pizza with a different cheese and top with a trellis of canned anchovy fillets or lean bacon strips and olives.

Cook in the oven for 25-35 minutes, until crisp and golden.

Serves 4-6.

Spinakopitta

155 g (5 oz) butter

250 g (8 oz) courgettes (zucchini), thinly sliced

500 g (1 lb) spinach, shredded

4 spring onions (shallots), thinly sliced

125 g (4 oz) marinated feta cheese (feta with oregano and olive oil), crumbled

2 eggs, beaten

black pepper, to taste

8 sheets filo pastry

Preheat oven to 180C (350F/ Gas 4).

In a saucepan, melt 30 g (1 oz) butter; sauté courgettes (zucchini) for 4 minutes. Turn into a large mixing bowl; add spinach and spring onions (shallots) and mix well. Add feta cheese, mix in eggs and season with pepper.

Melt remaining butter; liberally brush a deep 28 x 20 cm (11 x 8 in) baking tin. Line base and sides with 4 sheets of filo pastry, brushing each sheet with melted butter. Spoon vegetable mixture evenly over pastry base; cover with remaining 4 sheets of filo, brushing each with melted butter. Trim; tuck trimmings down inside dish to prevent filling escaping.

With a sharp knife, score top two layers of pastry into squares or diamonds. Cover with greaseproof paper and bake in the oven for about 45 minutes, until golden and crisp on top. Serve warm or cold, cut into shapes, with a mixed salad.

Serves 8.

Note: If marinated feta cheese is unobtainable, use plain feta and add 2 teaspoons olive oil and ½ teaspoon dried oregano when preparing filling.

Cheese & Mushroom Nests

250 g (8 oz) ready-made puff pastry
milk to glaze
1 teaspoon sesame seeds
SAUCE:
315 ml (10 fl oz/1¼ cups) milk
1 slice onion
6 peppercorns
1 bay leaf
pinch of ground mace
15 g (½ oz) butter
1 tablespoon plain flour
1 teaspoon dry mustard
2 tablespoons single (light) cream
60 g (2 oz) Leicester cheese, crumbled
FILLING:
2 teaspoons butter
2 shallots, chopped
125 g (4 oz/1 cup) sliced mushrooms.
2 tomatoes, skinned, seeded and sliced
1 tablespoon lemon juice
1 tablespoon snipped chives
8 fresh quail's eggs, hard-boiled

Preheat oven to 200 C (400F/Gas 6).

Roll out pastry and cut into four 10 cm (4 in) circles. Using a 5 cm (2 in) plain cutter, mark centres and press halfway through pastry. Rough up edge of each circle with a knife. Brush with milk and sprinkle with sesame seeds. Put on a dampened baking sheet and cook in the oven for 15-20 minutes, turning around once. Cool on a wire rack. Using a sharp knife, remove centre circles; discard.

Meanwhile, make sauce: in a saucepan, put milk, onion, peppercorns, bay leaf and mace. Bring to scalding point, then set aside for 10 minutes to infuse; strain.

In a clean pan, melt butter, stir in flour and gradually stir in milk. Bring to boil and boil for 1-2 minutes. Remove from heat. Add mustard, cream and cheese, cover and set aside on a very low heat.

To make filling, in a frying pan melt butter; add shallots and mushrooms and cook for 2 minutes. Add tomatoes and lemon juice and cook for 3 minutes; add chives. Immediately divide between pastry cases. Pour a little sauce over the top and put 2 quail's eggs on the sauce. Serve immediately with salad.

Serves 4.

Chicken & Brie Strudel Pies

3 cooked chicken breasts, skinned and thinly sliced
275 g (10 oz) blue Brie, rind removed, cut into small chunks
grated rind of 1 lemon
juice of ½ small lemon
½ teaspoon chopped thyme
6 teaspoons chopped parsley
60 g (2 oz) unsalted butter, melted
6 sheets filo pastry, halved

Preheat oven to 200 C (400F/Gas 6).

Mix together chicken, Brie, lemon rind and juice, thyme and parsley.

Brush insides of four 9 cm (3½ in) diameter dariole moulds with melted butter.

Brush one half sheet of filo pastry with butter. Place another half sheet on top at a 45° angle; brush with butter. Top with another half sheet at a 90° angle. Make a fist and mould pastry, butter side in, around it. Push well into a prepared mould, allowing surplus around top to stand proud of mould. Repeat with remaining sheets of filo.

Divide chicken mixture into 4 portions and use to fill pastry cases. Bring edges of pastry into centre one by one and seal together, but ensure points are sticking upright in a random way. Brush with any remaining butter. Place on a baking sheet and cook in the oven for 25 minutes.

Carefully tip filo packets out of the moulds, being very careful not to snap any of the fragile points. Place on baking sheet and return to oven for 5 minutes, to brown outer pastry.

Serve with buttered new potatoes and a mixed leaf salad.

Serves 4.

Goats' Cheese Soufflé

75 g (2½ oz) butter

60 g (2 oz/½ cup) plain flour

315 ml (10 fl oz/1¼ cups) milk

¼ teaspoon grated nutmeg

salt and pepper, to taste

4 eggs, separated

155 g (5 oz) goats' cheese, crumbled

TO GARNISH:

herbs

salad leaves

Evenly butter a 20 cm (8 in) soufflé dish and chill to let the butter harden. Preheat oven to 190C (375F/Gas 5) and place a baking sheet on middle shelf.

In a saucepan, melt 60 g (2 oz) butter, stir in flour and cook for 1 minute, stirring. Remove from heat and gradually blend in milk. Return to heat and cook, stirring, until sauce thickens. Remove from heat and stir in remaining butter, nutmeg and salt and pepper.

Leave to cool for a few minutes, then gradually beat in egg yolks. Stir in cheese; heat gently for 30 seconds to melt and blend into sauce.

In a bowl, whisk egg whites with a pinch of salt until stiff peaks form. Fold about one-quarter into cheese mixture until thoroughly incorporated; fold in remainder in three separate batches.

Pour mixture into chilled dish; it should half-fill dish. Put it on warmed baking sheet and bake in the oven for 30-40 minutes or until well risen and golden brown. Serve immediately, garnished with a few herbs and salad leaves.

Serves 4-5.

Note: To make individual soufflés divide the mixture between 4-5 individual soufflé dishes and bake for 15-20 minutes, until well risen and golden brown.

Cheese & Chive Choux Buns

PASTRY:

75 g (2½ oz/⅝ cup) plain flour

pinch each of salt and cayenne

30 g (1 oz/¼ cup) grated matured Cheddar

60 g (2 oz) butter

155 ml (5 fl oz/⅔ cup) water

2 eggs, beaten

FILLING:

60 g (2 oz) cream cheese with chives

185 g (6 oz) carrots, finely grated

SAUCE:

1 bunch watercress

75 ml (2½ fl oz/⅓ cup) milk

2 tablespoons single (light) cream

30 g (1 oz) cream cheese with chives

salt and pepper, to taste

TO GARNISH:

carrot 'flowers' or strips

few chives

sprigs of parsley

To make pastry, sift flour, salt and cayenne into a bowl. Mix in cheese. Put butter and water in a saucepan and slowly bring to boil. Remove from heat and immediately beat in flour mixture all at once. Return to low heat and beat vigorously until a soft ball forms and leaves the side of the pan. Cool slightly, then gradually add beaten eggs, beating between each addition. Continue beating until mixture is smooth and glossy; cover and leave until cold.

Preheat oven to 220C (425F/Gas 7). Pipe or spoon about 16 small mounds onto greased baking sheets. Bake in the oven for 15 minutes; lower temperature to 190C (375F/ Gas 5) and bake for a further 10-15 minutes, until well risen and golden. Transfer to a wire rack and slit the side of each bun. Leave to cool.

To make filling, blend cheese and carrot; spoon into choux buns.

To make sauce, put watercress, milk, cream and cheese in a blender or food processor and blend until smooth. Pour into a small saucepan and heat gently. Season to taste.

To serve, put 2 or 3 buns on each plate with a little sauce. Garnish with carrot, chives and parsley.

Makes 16.

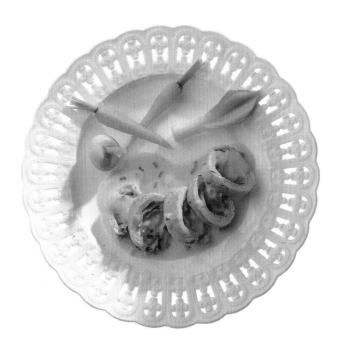

Gruyère and Chicken Roulade

4 chicken breasts, skinned
4 slices lean smoked ham
4 slices Gruyère cheese
4 tablespoons chopped chives
2 tablespoons olive oil
1 clove garlic, crushed
60 ml (2 fl oz/¼ cup) white wine
salt and pepper, to taste
155 ml (5 fl oz/⅔ cup) double
(thick) cream

Preheat oven to 180 C (350F/ Gas 4).

Slice three-quarters of the way horizontally through chicken breasts, cutting through the rounded edge; open out, cover with plastic wrap and beat with a rolling pin to flatten.

Cover each fillet with a slice of ham, then a slice of Gruyère. Set aside 1 tablespoon chives; sprinkle rest over cheese. Roll up chicken like a Swiss roll; secure with wooden cocktail sticks or string.

In an ovenproof pan, heat oil; cook chicken rolls gently, turning occasionally, until sealed. Pour off excess oil. Add garlic, wine and seasoning to pan, cover and cook in the oven for 25-30 minutes, until tender. Place roulades on a dish; remove cocktail sticks or string and keep warm.

Put pan on high heat and boil rapidly to reduce contents slightly; add cream and remaining chives and heat through.

Cut each chicken roulade into 1 cm (½ in) slices and arrange them overlapping on 4 warmed dinner plates. Pour over the sauce and serve immediately, with a selection of baby vegetables.

Serves 4.

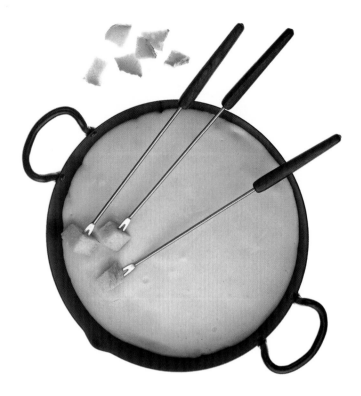

Fondue Suisse

1 clove garlic, halved
3 teaspoons cornflour
250 ml (8 fl oz/1 cup) dry white wine
250 g (8 oz) Gruyère cheese, diced
250 g (8 oz) Emmenthal cheese, diced
black pepper, to taste
3 tablespoons kirsch
1 baguette, cut into cubes

Rub cut garlic around the inside of an earthenware fondue dish or heavy-based pan; discard garlic.

Blend cornflour with a little of the wine. Pour remaining wine into pan and bring to boil. Add cheeses and stir until melted and blended.

Add blended cornflour and pepper and cook for about 2 minutes, until mixture combines and becomes creamy; do not allow to boil or the fondue will become stringy. Stir in kirsch.

To serve, keep fondue warm at the table. Divide bread cubes between 4 side plates for the diners, who dip bread into fondue using long-handled forks. Accompany with a chilled dry white wine.

Serves 4.

Garlic & Herb Fondue

1 clove garlic, halved
155 ml (5 fl oz/⅔ cup) dry white wine
3 teaspoons cornflour
315 ml (10 fl oz/1¼ cups) thick sour cream
2 x 150 g (5 oz) packets full fat soft cheese with garlic and herbs, e.g. Boursin
pinch of grated nutmeg
salt and pepper to taste
TO SERVE:
500 g (1 lb) cauliflower flowerets
500 g (1 lb) broccoli flowerets
chopped parsley
1 French stick, cubed and toasted

Rub cut garlic clove around inside of an earthenware fondue dish or heavy-based pan; discard garlic. Pour in 125 ml (4 fl oz/½ cup) wine; bring to boil. Blend cornflour with remaining wine; add to pan and cook, stirring constantly, until thickened. Reduce heat. Add thick sour cream and cheese; stir until cheese has melted. Add nutmeg, salt and pepper. Keep warm.

Bring a pan of salted water to the boil, add cauliflower and broccoli and boil for 5-6 minutes. Drain well and place in a warmed serving dish.

Sprinkle fondue with parsley and serve immediately, with the cauliflower and broccoli and bread cubes.

Serves 4-6.

Pine Nut, Pasta & Feta Salad

250 g (8 oz/1⅔ cups) pasta bows
6 bacon rashers, rinds removed
60 g (2 oz/½ cup) pine nuts
4 tomatoes, skinned, seeded and chopped
250 g (8 oz) feta cheese, cut into 1 cm (½ in) cubes
2 tablespoons torn basil leaves
DRESSING:
2 cloves garlic, crushed
2 tablespoons grated Parmesan cheese
2 tablespoons lemon or lime juice
4 tablespoons virgin olive oil
½ teaspoon Dijon mustard
salt and pepper, to taste
GARNISH:
sprigs of basil

Cook pasta in boiling salted water for 10 minutes or until *al dente*; drain under cold water; set aside.

Meanwhile, in a frying pan, cook bacon in its own fat until crispy; drain on absorbent kitchen paper, crumble and set aside. Remove all but 1 teaspoon of the bacon fat from frying pan. Add pine nuts to pan and fry until golden. Remove from pan and set aside.

To make dressing, combine all ingredients in a screw-top jar and shake until well blended.

Put tomatoes and cheese into a salad bowl; add bacon, pine nuts and basil and mix thoroughly. Pour over dressing and mix again. Garnish with basil sprigs.

Serves 4 as a main course; 6 as an accompaniment.

Note: This salad is best tossed in dressing about 20 minutes before serving, to allow flavours to develop.

Haloumi & Sesame Seed Salad

½ **head radicchio**
½ **curly endive**
½ **bunch watercress**
185 g (6 oz) **haloumi cheese**
1 **egg, beaten**
45 g (1½ oz/¾ cup) **fresh breadcrumbs**
oil for deep-frying
2 tablespoons **sesame seeds, toasted**
DRESSING:
3 tablespoons **virgin olive oil**
1 tablespoon **wine vinegar**
½ teaspoon **clear honey**
1 teaspoon **Dijon mustard**
1 clove **garlic, crushed**
salt and pepper, to taste
TO GARNISH (OPTIONAL):
nasturtium flowers

Break radicchio, curly endive and watercress into manageable pieces and put in a salad bowl.

To make dressing, mix all ingredients together with a small whisk until emulsified.

Cut cheese into 1 cm (½ in) cubes and dip into beaten egg; drain thoroughly. Put breadcrumbs in a polythene bag, add cheese cubes and toss to coat completely.

Heat oil in a deep-fryer and deep-fry cheese in batches until breadcrumbs turn golden brown; drain thoroughly on absorbent kitchen paper.

Pour dressing over salad and toss until well coated. Top with fried haloumi and sprinkle with toasted sesame seeds. Serve immediately, garnished with nasturtium flowers if desired.

Serves 4.

Grape & Gorgonzola Salad

½ small melon

8 Cos or Little Gem lettuce leaves

125 g (4 oz) seedless green grapes

90 g (3 oz) black grapes, seeded

90 g (3 oz) red grapes, seeded

DRESSING:

185 g (6 oz) Gorgonzola, crumbled

8 teaspoons mayonnaise

4 tablespoons Greek yogurt

1 teaspoon fruity sauce

¼ teaspoon chilli sauce

squeeze of lemon juice

GARNISH:

sprigs of parsley

few frisée and radicchio leaves

little paprika

First make dressing: combine all ingredients in a bowl; set aside. Cut melon into 4 slices; remove rind and seeds.

Place 2 lettuce leaves each on 4 individual plates. Arrange melon and grapes among the leaves.

Put a spoonful of dressing on top of each salad and garnish with parsley, frisée and radicchio leaves. Sprinkle a little paprika over dressing just before serving.

Serves 4.

Note: To make a thinner dressing if required, add a little single (light) cream or milk until the desired consistency is reached.

Rainbow Salad

1 small red pepper, seeded
1 small green pepper, seeded
1 small yellow pepper, seeded
1 small orange pepper, seeded
250 g (8 oz) mangetout (snow peas)
DRESSING:
90 g (3 oz) full fat soft cheese with garlic and herbs, e.g. Tartare
3 tablespoons crème fraîche or thick sour cream
1 tablespoon chopped mixed herbs
pinch of grated nutmeg
¼ teaspoon paprika (optional)
salt and pepper, to taste
GARNISH:
1 tablespoon chopped parsley
60 g (2 oz/½ cup) chopped walnuts
a little paprika (optional)

Cut all the peppers into julienne strips. Add the peppers and mangetout (snow peas) to a large pan of boiling water and boil for 2 minutes to blanch; drain and refresh in cold water. Arrange the vegetables attractively on a large salad platter, or in individual servings.

To make dressing: in a bowl, mix together cheese and crème fraîche or sour cream until evenly combined. Stir in herbs, nutmeg, and paprika if using. Add salt and pepper to taste. Spoon dressing on top of salad.

Mix together parsley and walnuts for the garnish and sprinkle on top of the salad. Sprinkle with a little paprika if desired. Serve immediately as an accompaniment, or with crusty bread as a light meal.

Serves 4-6

Orange & Hazelnut Crêpes

BATTER:

60 g (2 oz/½ cup) plain flour

1 small egg

155 ml (5 fl oz/⅔ cup) milk

pinch of grated nutmeg

2 drops of vanilla essence

finely grated rind of ½ orange

1 tablespoon oil for frying

TOPPING:

250 g (8 oz) Grand Marnier cheese

4 tablespoons crème fraîche

4 teaspoons finely shredded marmalade

2 oranges, peeled and segmented

SYRUP:

2 tablespoons maple syrup

4 tablespoons finely shredded marmalade

GARNISH:

shredded orange and lemon rind

chopped hazelnuts

To make batter, put all ingredients in a blender or food processor and blend until smooth. Heat a little oil in a small frying pan and pour in enough batter to make a pancake 8 cm (3 in) in diameter. Cook until bubbly on the surface and golden round the edge, then turn and cook the other side until golden. Turn onto greaseproof paper and keep warm while cooking remaining batter to make 16 pancakes in total.

To make topping, mix all ingredients, except the oranges, together in a bowl; set aside.

To make syrup, in a small saucepan, gently heat maple syrup and marmalade until melted and combined. Keep on a low heat while assembling pancakes.

Put 2 pancakes each on 4 individual plates. Put a spoonful of topping on them, arrange orange segments around, and pour a little syrup over cheese mixture. Decorate with orange and lemon shreds and nuts, and serve immediately.

Serves 4.

Note: If Grand Marnier cheese is unavailable, substitute 250 g (8 oz/1 cup) cream cheese and 4 teaspoons Grand Marnier liqueur; omit the crème fraîche.

Store any leftover pancakes, interleaved, in the freezer.

Wild Strawberry Cream

125 ml (4 fl oz/½ cup) double (thick) cream
3 tablespoons Framboise
1 tablespoon icing sugar, sifted
185 g (6 oz/¾ cup) fromage frais
185 g (6 oz) wild alpine strawberries
FROSTED LEAVES:
wild strawberry leaves
1 egg white
2 tablespoons caster sugar

In a bowl, whip cream, Framboise and icing sugar together until it forms fairly stiff peaks. Fold in fromage frais and all but 12 strawberries. Spoon into pretty glasses and chill for 30 minutes.

To make frosted leaves, brush leaves very lightly on both sides with a little egg white; sprinkle with caster sugar, making sure they are completely coated. Leave in a warm place for 30 minutes to dry.

Decorate the creams with remaining strawberries and frosted leaves. Serve with crisp wafer dessert biscuits.

Serves 4.

Note: Frosted leaves will last for up to 2 weeks in an airtight container if they are completely coated.

Variation: Use ordinary strawberries instead of wild alpine strawberries and slice them.

Raspberries may also be used, in place of strawberries, with frosted raspberry leaves to decorate.

Blueberry Waffles

BATTER:

375 g (12 oz/3 cups) plain flour

pinch of salt

1 teaspoon bicarbonate of soda

1 teaspoon baking powder

2 large eggs

250 ml (8 fl oz/1 cup) milk

about 125 ml (4 fl oz/½ cup) cold water

125 g (4 oz) butter, melted

TOPPING:

125 g (4 oz) Petit Suisse cheese

6 teaspoons whipped cream

60 g (2 oz/⅓ cup) icing sugar, sifted

125 g (4 oz/1 cup) blueberries

First prepare topping. Blend together cheese, cream and icing sugar; set aside.

To make batter, sift dry ingredients into a bowl. Beat eggs and milk together, then gently stir in to dry ingredients to form a heavy batter. Gradually add sufficient water to make a batter thick enough to coat the back of the spoon; add butter and mix to blend.

Heat an electric waffle iron and brush both sides with oil. Fill one side with batter, clamp down lid and cook until steam ceases to escape and waffles are golden brown and crisp. Remove from iron and keep warm while cooking next waffle.

To serve, put a spoonful of prepared topping on each waffle and cover with blueberries. Serve hot.

Makes 2-3.

Note: Non-electric waffle irons must be turned over halfway through cooking to ensure even results.

Pashka

250 g (8 oz/1 cup) cottage cheese
75 ml (2½ fl oz/⅓ cup) double (thick) cream
1 egg yolk
60 g (2 oz/¼ cup) caster sugar
30 g (1 oz/¼ cup) raisins
30 g (1 oz/¼ cup) finely chopped dried apricots
15 g (½ oz/6 teaspoons) chopped mixed nuts (e.g. walnuts, hazelnuts, almonds)
few drops vanilla essence
125 g (4 oz) unsalted butter
TO DECORATE:
fresh fruit in season

Rub cottage cheese through a fine nylon sieve. Put into a large saucepan with remaining ingredients and heat gently for 3-4 minutes, stirring constantly; do not allow to boil.

Remove from heat and leave until thickened and completely cold.

Pour into prepared container (see below) and put on a rack in a dish, or in a jug which is just big enough to leave a space underneath to catch drips. Chill for about 8 hours, until fully drained.

Turn out onto a serving dish and decorate with fresh fruit.

Serves 4.

Note: Pashka is traditionally made in a flowerpot-shaped mould; use a new plastic or clay flowerpot. Alternatively, a sieve or strainer can be used to achieve the required rounded shape. Line chosen mould with cheesecloth or muslin, or use a clean tea-towel if unavailable.

Deep-baked Cheesecake

125 g (4 oz) butter or margarine

250 g (8 oz) sweetmeal digestive biscuits (granita), finely crushed

125 g (4 oz/⅓ cup) raspberry jam

185 g (6 oz/¾ cup) fromage frais

185 g (6 oz/¾ cup) cottage cheese

4 eggs, separated

60 ml (2 fl oz/¼ cup) double (thick) cream

125 g (4 oz/½ cup) caster sugar

60 g (2 oz/½ cup) plain flour

juice and grated rind of 1 small lemon

TO DECORATE:

lemon slices

pared lemon rind

Preheat oven to 160C (325F/ Gas 3).

In a small saucepan, melt butter or margarine; stir in biscuit crumbs. Press onto base of a 20.5 cm (8 in) square, loose-bottomed cake tin. In a small saucepan, warm jam slightly to melt; spread over biscuit base. Lightly butter sides of tin.

In a blender or food processor, thoroughly blend cheeses, egg yolks, cream, sugar and flour. Add lemon juice and rind and blend or process briefly.

In a bowl, whisk egg whites until stiff; fold into cheese mixture with a metal spoon. Pour onto biscuit base and bake in the oven for 45 minutes to 1 hour or until brown on top and firm to touch. Switch off heat; leave cake in oven for 1-2 hours or until cool. Remove from oven and leave in tin until completely cold.

To serve, cut into 4 slices, then cut each slice in half. Decorate with lemon slices and twists of lemon rind.

Serves 8.

Chocolate Truffle Cheesecake

12-14 sponge fingers

6 teaspoons brandy or rum

250 g (8 oz/1 cup) cream cheese

250 ml (8 fl oz/1 cup) double (thick) cream

few drops vanilla essence

350 g (12 oz) plain (dark) chocolate, melted

2 egg whites

TO DECORATE:

60 g (2 oz) milk chocolate, melted

60 g (2 oz) white chocolate, melted

rose leaves

1 teaspoon cocoa powder

Line the base of an 18 cm (7 in) springform cake tin with non-stick paper.

Arrange sponge fingers over base, cutting them as necessary to fit as tightly as possible. Spoon over brandy or rum.

Beat together cream cheese and cream until thick; stir in vanilla essence and cooled chocolate and mix well.

In a bowl, whisk egg whites until stiff; fold into cheese mixture. Spoon into prepared tin, level the top and chill for at least 6 hours.

To prepare decoration, brush melted milk and white chocolate onto underside of rose leaves using a fine paintbrush. Place chocolate side up on non-stick paper and allow to set. Apply a second coat and leave to dry. Carefully lift tip of leaves and peel away from chocolate.

Invert cake onto a serving plate. Arrange chocolate leaves over the top. Using a fine sieve, dust cocoa powder around outside top edge.

Serves 6-10.

Note: This dessert is deceptively rich so serve in small pieces.

Viennese Peach Crescents

125 g (4 oz/1 cup) plain flour
125 g (4 oz) unsalted butter, chilled and cut into 8 pieces
125 g (4 oz/½ cup) curd cheese, beaten lightly to soften
250 g (8 oz) peach conserve
1 egg yolk beaten with 2 teaspoons milk, to glaze
GLACÉ ICING:
90 g (3 oz/½ cup) icing sugar
1-2 teaspoons water

Sift flour into a mixing bowl. Add butter, scooping flour over each piece to keep separate. Using two round-bladed table knives, continue cutting in butter until pieces are size of small cherries; it should remain in small lumps not completely blended into flour. Add cheese and mix to form a dough which just holds together; gather into a ball. Wrap in plastic wrap and chill for at least 20 minutes.

On a lightly floured surface, cut pastry in half and roll out each piece to 3 mm (⅛ in) thickness. Cut into 5 cm (2 in) squares, then roll out into very thin 8 cm (3 in) squares. Place a spoonful of conserve on one corner of each square; roll up diagonally from this corner to form a sausage shape. With triangular centre flap underneath, curve pastries into crescents. Place well apart on an ungreased baking sheet. Brush with beaten egg yolk. Chill for at least 30 minutes, until firm.

Preheat oven to 180C (350F/ Gas 4).

To make glacé icing, sift icing sugar into a bowl. Gradually stir in enough water to make a very thick icing.

Bake pastries in the oven for 15-20 minutes or until risen and golden brown. Using a greaseproof paper piping bag with the end snipped off, pipe a little glacé icing on top of warm pastries. Serve warm.

Makes 16-20.

Pineapple Passion Cake

3 pineapple slices, fresh or canned
250 g (8 oz) butter or soft margarine
250 g (8 oz/1¼ cups) caster sugar
3 eggs, beaten
250 g (8 oz/2 cups) self-raising flour
1 teaspoon baking powder
315 g (10 oz) carrot, grated
155 g (5 oz/1¼ cups) finely chopped pecans or walnuts
6 teaspoons lemon juice
ICING:
375 g (12 oz/1½ cups) full fat soft cream cheese, e.g. Philadelphia
90 g (3 oz/½ cup) icing sugar, sifted
3 teaspoons clear honey

Grease a 20 cm (7 in) round deep cake tin or ring mould. Preheat oven to 350C (180F/Gas 4).

Finely chop one pineapple slice. Divide the other two into tiny wedges and set aside for decoration.

In a bowl, beat butter or margarine and caster sugar together until light and fluffy. Gradually beat in eggs, a little at a time. Sift flour and baking powder together; fold into creamed mixture. Stir in chopped pineapple, carrot, three quarters of the nuts and 3 teaspoons lemon juice.

Pour mixture into prepared tin and bake in the oven for about 1¼ hours, until golden and a skewer inserted in the centre comes out clean; lower the temperature to 325C (160F/Gas 3) if the cake is becoming too brown. Cool on a wire rack.

To make the icing, cream together cheese, icing sugar, honey and remaining lemon juice and spread over the top and side of cake. Decorate with remaining nuts and reserved pineapple wedges. Leave to stand for a few hours before serving.

Serves 8-10.

Cheese & Mustard Bread

15 g (½ oz/3 teaspoons) fresh yeast
315 ml (10 fl oz/1¼ cups) warm water
250 g (8 oz/1¾ cups) rye flour
250 g (8 oz/2 cups) plain strong bread flour
1 teaspoon salt
1 tablespoon oil
6 tablespoons whole grain mustard
185 g (6 oz/1½ cups) grated Emmenthal cheese
3 tablespoons chopped parsley
1 teaspoon black mustard seeds

Cream yeast with a little of the water; leave until frothy. Put flours and salt in a bowl; make a well in the centre. Add yeast mixture, remaining water and oil and mix to a soft dough.

Knead on a lightly floured surface for about 5 minutes, until smooth and elastic. Put into a clean bowl, cover with a damp tea-towel and leave to rise in a warm place for 1½-2 hours, until doubled in size.

Preheat oven to 220C (425F/Gas 7).

Knead dough again for 2 minutes, then roll into a 30.5 cm (12 in) square. Spread with mustard, then sprinkle with cheese and parsley.

Roll up like a Swiss roll and place, join side down, on a floured baking sheet; brush with water and sprinkle with mustard seeds.

Bake in the oven for 10 minutes; lower temperature to 200C (400F/Gas 6) and bake for 20 minutes, until bread sounds hollow when tapped underneath. Cool on a wire rack.

Makes 1 loaf.

Variation: Use a light beer instead of water.

Haloumi & Mint Bread

15 g (½ oz/3 teaspoons) fresh yeast
315 ml (10 fl oz/1¼ cups) warm water
250 g (8 oz/1¾ cups) wholewheat flour
250 g (8 oz/2 cups) plain flour
1 teaspoon salt
1 tablespoon olive oil
175 (6 oz) haloumi cheese, diced
3 tablespoons chopped mint
1 tablespoon sesame seeds

Cream yeast with a little of the water; leave until frothy. Put flours and salt in a bowl; make a well in the centre. Add yeast mixture, remaining water and oil and mix to a soft dough.

Knead on a lightly floured surface for about 5 minutes, until smooth and elastic. Put into a clean bowl, cover with a damp tea-towel and leave to rise in a warm place for 1½-2 hours, until doubled in size.

Preheat oven to 230C (450F/ Gas 8). Turn dough onto a floured surface and punch into a flattish round. Put cheese and mint on top, fold over and knead for about 5 minutes, until it is well mixed in.

Shape into a circle and press out into a 20.5 cm (8 in) round. Put on a floured baking sheet and make a cut 2.5 cm (1 in) from the edge, right through to the bottom, all the way round. Brush with water and sprinkle with sesame seeds.

Bake in the oven for 10 minutes; lower temperature to 200C (400F/ Gas 6) and bake for 20 minutes, until bread sounds hollow when tapped underneath.

Cool on a wire rack.

Makes 1 loaf.